Better Homes and Gardens®

A Cross-Stitch CHRISTMAS

Handmade Treasures

BETTER HOMES AND GARDENS® BOOKS

Des Moines, Iowa

BETTER HOMES AND GARDENS® BOOKS
An Imprint of Meredith® Books

A CROSS-STITCH CHRISTMAS
Vice President and Editorial Director: Elizabeth P. Rice
Editor-in-Chief: Carol Field Dahlstrom
Managing Editor: Susan Banker
Art Director: Gayle Schadendorf
Copy Chief: Eve Mahr
Senior Writer: Barbara Hickey
Senior Graphic Designer: Bridget Sandquist
Technical Editor: Colleen Johnson
Administrative Assistant: Peggy Daugherty
Contributing Technical Illustrator: Chris Neubauer
Production Manager: Douglas Johnston

President, Book Group: Joseph J. Ward
Vice President, Retail Marketing: Jamie L. Martin
Vice President, Direct Marketing: Timothy Jarrell
Publisher, Craftways: Maureen Ruth

Meredith Corporation
Chairman of the Executive Committee: E.T. Meredith III
Chairman of the Board and Chief Executive Officer: Jack D. Rehm
President and Chief Operating Officer: William T. Kerr

All of us at Better Homes and Gardens® Books are dedicated to providing you with the information and ideas you need to create beautiful and useful projects. We guarantee your satisfaction with this book for as long as you own it. We welcome your questions, comments, or suggestions. Please write to us at: Cross Stitch & Country Crafts®, Better Homes and Gardens® Books, RW 235, 1716 Locust Street, Des Moines, IA 50309-3023.

If you would like to order additional copies of any of our books, call 1-800-678-2803 or check with your local bookstore.

Cover: Photograph by Hopkins Associates

Our "Mark of Excellence" craft seal assures you that every project in this publication has been constructed and checked under the direction of the crafts experts at Better Homes and Gardens® Cross Stitch & Country Crafts® magazine.

*There's no better time than Christmas to extend
affectionate tokens of friendship and love. As stitchers,
we are filled with joy as we present beautifully wrapped
gifts to family and friends — special remembrances
we have lovingly stitched throughout the year.*

*The inspiring collection of cross-stitch projects
you'll find in this book will help you express all those
heartfelt sentiments with clever gift ideas and
fun-to-stitch fashion designs as well as decorations
for your own holiday home.*

*May Christmastime bring you and your family
all the love and joy your hearts can hold. And may the
pages of this festive cross-stitch book help you share the
wondrous magic of the season by creating your
very own Handmade Treasures.*

A Cross-Stitch CHRISTMAS

Trim the Tree

The wonderful tradition of trimming the Christmas tree is the inspiration for these treasured cross-stitch decorations.

Welcoming Wreaths

Friends and family will feel right at home when greeted with these lovely symbols of the season.

Stockings for Santa

Both the young and the young at heart will anticipate St. Nick's arrival with these creative stocking designs.

Heartwarming Gifts

Touch the heart of those you love with these fun-to-stitch gift ideas that would be appreciated any time of the year.

Festive Fashion

Catch the spirit of the season by getting all decked out in spectacular holiday fashions you can stitch yourself.

All Through the House

Make the season even brighter by creating a holiday home that will be remembered for many Christmases to come.

Trim the Tree

Each year treasured Christmas decorations are carefully unwrapped and proudly displayed as family and friends gather together for the holidays. From a child's first paper chain garland to prized heirloom ornaments, each lovingly crafted piece preserves a moment in time. Whether you prefer homespun country or elegant Victorian, you are sure to find a new favorite in this glorious collection of Christmas trims.

Guiding Star Tree Topper

Radiant beams from the Star of Bethlehem guided the Wise Men on their Christmas journey. This elegant star tree topper recreates that radiance with metallic stitches accented by rows of gleaming beads. Rich gold lace encircles this dazzling star which will provide a brilliant crowning touch to your tree. Complete instructions and chart begin on page 15.

DESIGNER: SUSAN CORNELISON ● PHOTOGRAPHER: HOPKINS ASSOCIATES

Trim the Tree

Frosted Snowflakes

No two frosty snowflakes are alike, but below are two cross-stitched versions you can duplicate time and time again and enjoy always! Delicate silver threads accent the cotton cross-stitches in these shimmering snowflake ornaments. Silver sequin trim and tassels made of pearl cotton and silver cable are the perfect complement to these sparkling designs. Complete instructions and charts begin on page 17.

DESIGNER: KATHY ZEITMAN ● PHOTOGRAPHER: HOPKINS ASSOCIATES

Glorious Angel Tree Topper

This glittering angel with her flowing gown and luminescent wings will hold a place of honor on your tree. With a glowing candle to guide her, our angel tree topper glistens with metallic threads that add a heavenly luster to the delicate shades of her rose-trimmed gown. For a festive decorating idea, slip our angel topper over a small jar and surround it with greens to create an elegant holiday centerpiece. Instructions and chart begin on page 18.

DESIGNER: URSULA MICHAEL ● PHOTOGRAPHER: HOPKINS ASSOCIATES

Festive Stocking Garland and Gift Tags and Holly Jolly Tree Skirt

Treat your family to a real homespun Christmas by trimming your tree with these charming decorations. Miniature stockings and bright red wooden beads are strung on jute twine to create a festive holiday garland. The stocking designs are also stitched on perforated paper to make matching gift tags. The tree with all its fancy trimmings is skirted with a jute tree skirt cross-stitched with metallic gold and wool yarns and finished with a generous ruffling of red and green satin ribbons. Complete instructions and charts for these designs begin on page 20.

DESIGNERS: TREE SKIRT, NANCY MARSHALL; GARLAND AND TAGS, ALICE OKON PHOTOGRAPHER: HOPKINS ASSOCIATES

Lacy Hardanger Ornaments

Each of these lovely Hardanger ornaments is a tiny treasure delicately stitched using white pearl cotton. The diamond-shaped ornament is stitched on white Lugana fabric with a spectacular center made of needleweaving and webs. Stitched on silver and white Valerie fabric, the sweet angel ornament captures a heavenly feeling with its beautiful angel charm. Complete instructions and charts begin on page 24.

DESIGNER: ROSALYN WATNEMO
PHOTOGRAPHER: HOPKINS ASSOCIATES

Scandinavian Mitten Ornaments

The simple charm of these tiny cross-stitched mittens makes them a holiday favorite. Embellished with beads and red and green cords, these tiny mitten ornaments are stitched over two threads on 32-count ivory Jobelan fabric. Complete instructions and charts are on page 23.

DESIGNER: ROBIN CLARK
PHOTOGRAPHER: SCOTT LITTLE

Celestial Wonders

Golden threads stitched on perforated plastic turn these playful celestial designs into striking ornaments. The same eye-catching motifs work beautifully to personalize a purchased robe or baby sleeper. The sun design is stitched, then appliquéd on Dad's robe—the baby's sleeper motif is worked on waste canvas. Instructions and charts begin on page 25.

DESIGNER: CAROLE RODGERS ● PHOTOGRAPHER: HOPKINS ASSOCIATES

Trim the Tree

Merry Santa Ornament and Shirt

Santa sports a Southwestern look in this colorful design. A triangle border with candy canes and Christmas trees surrounds the center motif. Work it over two threads on 28-count fabric as a charming ornament or create a very different look by stitching the design on a sweatshirt using waste canvas. Chart and complete instructions for both versions of this design are on page 27.

DESIGNER: SHARON MANN ● PHOTOGRAPHER: HOPKINS ASSOCIATES

★★★GUIDING STAR TREE TOPPER

As shown on page 7, finished topper measures 10¼x8½ inches.

MATERIALS

FABRICS
12x10-inch piece of 28-count white Jubilee fabric

12x10-inch piece of lightweight fusible interfacing

15x10-inch piece of white cotton fabric

THREADS
Cotton embroidery floss in colors listed in key on page 17

Blending filament in colors listed in key on page 17

SUPPLIES
Needle

Embroidery hoop

Mill Hill seed beads and bugle beads as listed in key on page 17

11x8½ piece of tracing paper

25-inch piece of purchased gold metallic piping

Two 12x9-inch pieces of clear perforated plastic for stabilizers

6-inch piece of white bias tape

27-inch piece of ⅞-inch-wide gold flat lace

INSTRUCTIONS

Tape or zigzag the edges of the Jubilee fabric to prevent fraying. Find the center of chart and the center of fabric; begin stitching there.

Use three plies of floss to work cross-stitches over two threads of fabric. Work blended needle as specified in key. Work backstitches using one ply of floss or one strand of filament.

Use one ply of dark tan floss to sew seed beads and bugle beads to design. Fuse the interfacing to the back of the finished stitchery following the manufacturer's instructions.

Fold tracing paper in half lengthwise. Match paper fold to center line on pattern, *right*, and transfer pattern onto tracing paper; cut out. Pattern includes ¼-inch seam allowances.

Center pattern over stitched design; cut out. Baste piping around stitched design with raw edges even. Using full pattern, cut one top back piece from cotton fabric and one front stabilizer from plastic. Cut pattern on fold line for back. Use top of pattern to cut one back stabilizer from plastic. Use bottom of pattern to cut bottom back piece from cotton fabric. Trim away ¼ inch on the curved edges of both plastic pieces.

Stitch bias tape along straight edge of bottom back; trim ends of bias tape to match curves. Set aside.

Fold under bottom section of top back as indicated on pattern; press. Baste the top and bottom back pieces to front piece, right sides together. Stitch along basting lines. Clip the curves, turn, and press.

Insert front stabilizer into star with bottom of plastic behind bottom back fabric. Insert back stabilizer into star with straight edge inside fold. Glue lace around the back edge of tree topper.

**STAR
TREE TOPPER
Cut 1 from cotton
Cut 1 from plastic
Cut 1 to fold line from plastic**

Center

Fold line for back

**Cut 1 to fold line
from cotton**

Trim the Tree

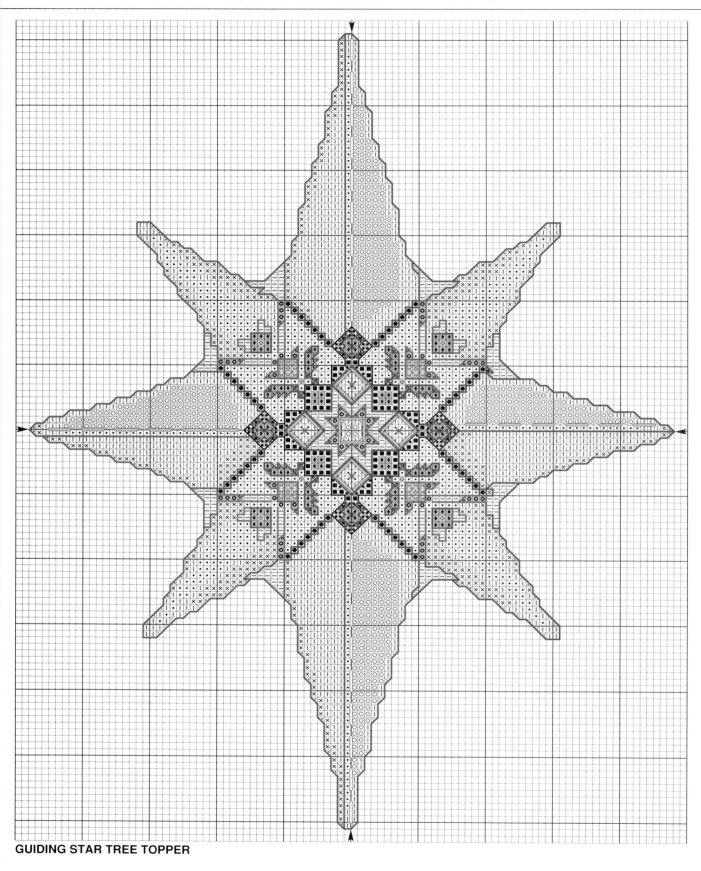

GUIDING STAR TREE TOPPER

GUIDING STAR TREE TOPPER

ANCHOR		DMC	
875	−	503	True blue green
308	●	782	Topaz

BLENDED NEEDLE

1006	◆	304	Christmas red (1X) and
		003HL	Kreinik red blending filament (2X)
403	■	310	Black (1X) and
		005HL	Kreinik black blending filament (2X)
1045	☒	436	Dark tan (1X) and
		002	Kreinik gold blending filament (2X)
878	◉	501	Dark blue green (1X) and
		009HL	Kreinik emerald blending filament (2X)
891	○	676	Light old gold (1X) and
		002HL	Kreinik gold blending filament (2X)
890	⊡	729	Medium old gold (1X) and
		002HL	Kreinik gold blending filament (2X)
885	•	739	Pale tan (1X) and
		002	Kreinik gold blending filament (2X)

BACKSTITCH

1006	╱	304	Christmas red – center detail
403	╱	310	Black – center detail
359	╱	801	Coffee brown – star
	╱	009HL	Kreinik emerald blending filament – center detail

SEED BEADS

	×	0215	Sea blue – centers of bugle bead diamonds
	×	00557	Gold – ice green cluster centers, red square centers
	×	00561	Ice green – center clusters
	×	03003	Antique cranberry – centers of red and black squares

BUGLE BEADS

| | ▯ | 72010 | Ice – vertical star points |
| | ▯ | 72011 | Victorian gold – horizontal star points, center motif |

Stitch count: 122 high x 96 wide

Finished design sizes:
14-count fabric – 8³⁄₄ x 6⁷⁄₈ inches
11-count fabric – 11¹⁄₈ x 8³⁄₄ inches
16-count fabric – 7⁵⁄₈ x 6 inches

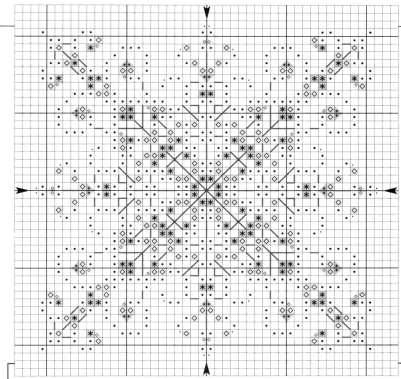

BLACK SNOWFLAKE ORNAMENT

BLENDED NEEDLE

ANCHOR		DMC	
002	•	000	White (2X) and 001C Kreinik silver cord (1X)
175	✳	794	Cornflower blue (2X) and 001C Kreinik silver cord (1X)
1031	◇	3753	Antique blue (2X) and 001C Kreinik silver cord (1X)

BACKSTITCH

| | ╱ | 001C Kreinik silver cord (1X) |

Stitch count: 44 high x 44 wide

Finished design sizes:
14-count fabric – 3¹⁄₈ x 3¹⁄₈ inches
16-count fabric – 2³⁄₄ x 2³⁄₄ inches
18-count fabric – 2³⁄₈ x 2³⁄₈ inches

BLUE SNOWFLAKE ORNAMENT

BLENDED NEEDLE

ANCHOR		DMC	
002	•	000	White (2X) and 001C Kreinik silver cord (1X)
891	☒	676	Light old gold (2X) and 001C Kreinik silver cord (1X)
886	○	677	Pale old gold (2X) and 001C Kreinik silver cord (1X)

BACKSTITCH

| | ╱ | 001C Kreinik silver cord (1X) |

Stitch count: 44 high x 44 wide

Finished design sizes:
14-count fabric – 3¹⁄₈ x 3¹⁄₈ inches
16-count fabric – 2³⁄₄ x 2³⁄₄ inches
18-count fabric – 2³⁄₈ x 2³⁄₈ inches

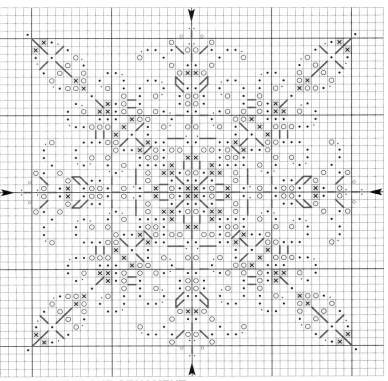

BLUE SNOWFLAKE ORNAMENT

Trim the Tree

⋆⋆FROSTED SNOWFLAKES

As shown on page 8, finished ornaments measure 5¾x5¾ inches.

MATERIALS
For each ornament
FABRICS
6x6-inch piece of black or dark blue 14-count Aida cloth
5x5-inch piece of black or blue felt
THREADS
Cotton embroidery floss in colors listed in key on page 17
Silver cord as listed in key on page 17
One skein of black (DMC 310) or royal blue (DMC 820) #5 pearl cotton
Two spools of Kreinik 001P silver cable
SUPPLIES
Needle; embroidery hoop
Crafts glue
4x4-inch piece of self-stick mounting board with foam
4x4-inch piece of self-stick mounting board
3-inch-wide piece of cardboard
½ yard of ½-inch-wide silver braid trim
⅓ yard of ¹⁄₁₆-inch-diameter silver cord

INSTRUCTIONS
Tape or zigzag edges of fabric to prevent fraying. Find center of chart and of fabric; begin stitching there. Work all stitches as specified in key. Press finished stitchery from back.

Peel protective paper from back of foam mounting board. Center the foam side on back of stitched design and press to stick. Trim fabric to ½ inch beyond edge of mounting board. Fold fabric edges to back; glue with crafts glue, mitering corners as needed. Repeat with felt and remaining mounting board.

For tassel, thread needle with a 6-inch length of coordinating pearl cotton; set aside. Wrap one strand each of pearl cotton and cable around cardboard 100 times. Thread 6-inch strand of pearl cotton under wound loops at one edge; tie. Cut loops on opposite edge; remove cardboard.

Tie a second 6-inch strand of pearl cotton around tassel ½ inch below tied end. Glue a 2-inch piece of braid around tassel over pearl cotton. Trim ends evenly. Glue ends of first 6-inch strand to back of design at a corner.

For hanger, fold 12-inch piece of silver cord in half and knot ends. Glue ends to back of stitched design on the corner opposite the tassel.

Glue back sides of mounting cardboard squares together. Dab glue on ends of braid to prevent fraying. Beginning at one corner, glue braid around edge of ornament.

⋆⋆⋆GLORIOUS ANGEL TREE TOPPER

As shown on page 9, finished tree topper measures 10¾x8½ inches.

MATERIALS
FABRICS
14x12-inch piece of 28-count white linen
12x9-inch piece of clear perforated plastic
12x9-inch piece of fleece
12x9-inch piece of white felt
THREADS
Cotton embroidery floss and #8 braid in colors listed in key
Blending filament in colors listed in key
SUPPLIES
Needle; embroidery hoop
Tracing paper; pencil
1 yard of pre-gathered ½-inch-wide silver lace
6-inch piece of ¼-inch-wide elastic

INSTRUCTIONS
Tape or zigzag edges of fabric. Find center of chart and of fabric; begin stitching there. Use two plies of floss to work cross-stitches over two threads of fabric. Work blended needle and backstitches as specified in the key. Press stitchery from back.

Trace outline of stitchery on paper. Cut paper pattern ¼ inch larger, as indicated by dotted line on chart. Use pattern to cut one shape each from plastic, fleece, and felt. Center felt on stitchery; cut out linen ½ inch beyond felt pattern.

Glue fleece to plastic; center stitchery over fleece. Fold excess fabric to back, clip, and glue. Glue lace around edge, overlapping ends at bottom. Glue felt to back. Fold ends of elastic under; tack to sides 4 inches from bottom.

GLORIOUS ANGEL TREE TOPPER		
ANCHOR		DMC
008	▲	353 Dark peach
217	●	367 Dark pistachio green
214	⊡	368 Light pistachio green
1046	◪	435 True golden brown
362	➕	437 Medium tan
136	★	799 Medium Delft blue
144	◉	800 Pale Delft blue
033	▼	892 Medium carnation
027	▢	894 Pale carnation
1011	⊟	948 Light peach
120	#	3747 Pale periwinkle
1037	▽	3756 Pale baby blue
	♡	9100 Kreinik sunlight #8 braid (1X)
	◎	002 Kreinik gold #8 braid (1X)
BLENDED NEEDLE		
002	⊡	000 White (2X) and 095 Kreinik starburst filament (1X)
1017	✕	316 Medium antique mauve (2X) and 042 Kreinik confetti fuchsia filament (1X)
9046	▶	321 True Christmas red (2X) and 003 Kreinik red filament (1X)
228	◆	700 Medium Christmas green (2X) and 008HL Kreinik green filament (1X)
302	⊞	743 Medium yellow (2X) and 091 Kreinik star yellow filament (1X)
300	▷	745 Pale yellow (2X) and 091 Kreinik star yellow filament (1X)
275	◩	746 Off white (2X) and 091 Kreinik star yellow filament (1X)
024	⊗	776 Medium pink (2X) and 095 Kreinik starburst filament (1X)
1016	▢	778 Pale antique mauve (2X) and 042 Kreinik confetti fuchsia filament (1X)
271	◩	819 Light pink (2X) and 095 Kreinik starburst filament (1X)
292	△	3078 Pale lemon (2X) and 095 Kreinik starburst filament (1X)
BACKSTITCH		
352	╱	300 Deep mahogany (1X)— facial features, hands, hair
042	╱	309 Dark rose (2X)— dress, lips
1005	╱	498 Dark Christmas red (2X)— roses
907	╱	832 Medium bronze (1X)— candle flame
236	╱	3799 Dark charcoal (1X)—eyes
	╱	042 Kreinik confetti fuchsia filament (2X)—snowflakes on skirt, veins on wings
	╱	329 Kreinik Bahama blue filament (2X)—lines on petticoat

18

GLORIOUS ANGEL TREE TOPPER

Stitch count: *141 high x 109 wide*
Finished design sizes:
14-count fabric – 10¼ x 7¾ inches
16-count fabric – 8⅞ x 6⅝ inches
18-count fabric – 7⅞ x 6¼ inches

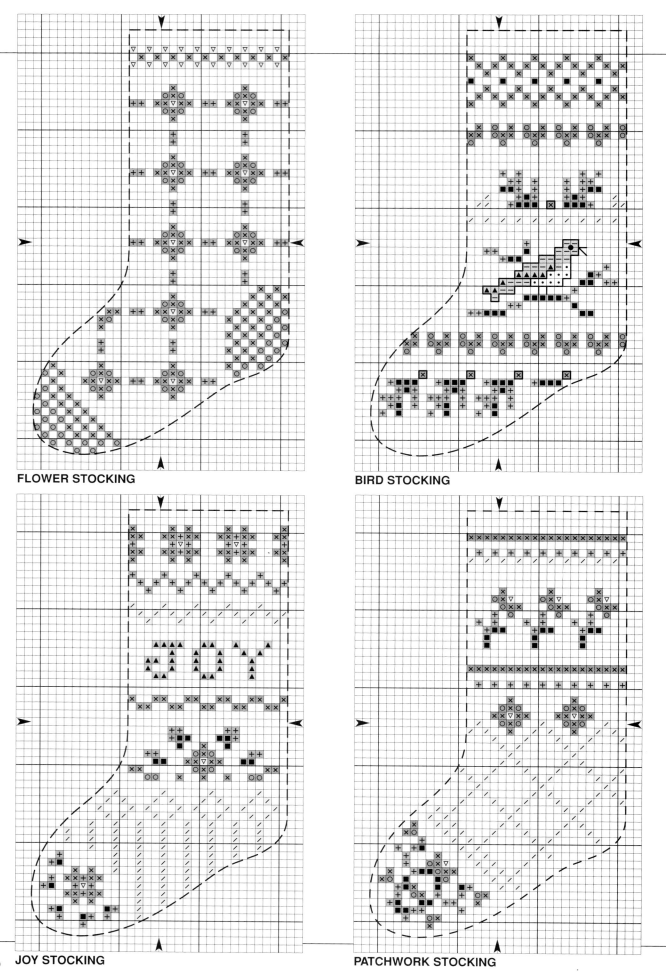

FLOWER STOCKING

BIRD STOCKING

JOY STOCKING

PATCHWORK STOCKING

STOCKING GARLAND AND GIFT TAGS

ANCHOR		DMC
387	·	Ecru
9046	⊠	321 Christmas red
891	╱	676 Old gold
305	▽	725 Topaz
1005	◉	816 Garnet
161	▲	826 Bright blue
229	■	910 True emerald
209	⊞	912 Light emerald
928	⊟	3761 Sky blue

BACKSTITCH

403	╱	310 Black – bird legs
9046	╱	321 Christmas red – berries
891	╱	676 Old gold – bird beak
161	╱	826 Bright blue – bird

FRENCH KNOT

403	●	310 Black – bird eye

FLOWER STOCKING stitch count:
53 high x 32 wide

FLOWER STOCKING finished design sizes:
11-count fabric – 4⅞ x 2⅞ inches
14-count fabric – 3⅞ x 2¼ inches

BIRD STOCKING stitch count:
47 high x 31 wide

BIRD STOCKING finished design sizes:
11-count fabric – 4¼ x 2¾ inches
14-count fabric – 3⅜ x 2¼ inches

JOY STOCKING stitch count:
52 high x 31 wide

JOY STOCKING finished design sizes:
11-count fabric – 4¾ x 2¾ inches
14-count fabric – 3¾ x 2¼ inches

PATCHWORK STOCKING stitch count:
51 high x 31 wide

PATCHWORK STOCKING finished design sizes:
11-count fabric – 4⅝ x 2¾ inches
14-count fabric – 3⅝ x 2¼ inches

★★STOCKING GARLAND

As shown on pages 10–11, finished stockings measure 4¾x3 inches.

MATERIALS

FABRICS *for each stocking*
6x6-inch piece of 11-count white Aida cloth
6x4-inch piece of red cotton fabric
FLOSS
Cotton embroidery floss in colors listed in key
SUPPLIES
Needle; embroidery hoop
Tapestry needle; erasable marker
5-inch piece of red rattail cord
Crafts glue; jute twine
¼-inch-diameter red wood beads

INSTRUCTIONS

Tape or zigzag edges of fabric. Find center of chart and of fabric; begin stitching there. Use three plies of floss to work cross-stitches and one ply to work French knots and backstitches. Use marker to draw stocking outline as shown by dotted line on chart. Cut out ¼ inch beyond outline. Stitch desired number of stockings.

Use stitched stocking shape as a pattern to cut a back from red fabric. Sew stocking front to back, right sides facing using ¼-inch seams and leaving top open; turn. Fold top edges to inside; press. Fold a 4½-inch piece of cord to form a loop; tack to top right edge of stocking. Tie a small jute bow onto cord at stocking top. Thread jute through a bead, then through stocking loop; tie loop to cord. Alternate beads and stockings every 2½ inches until desired length is reached.

★★STOCKING GIFT TAGS

As shown on pages 10–11, finished tags measure 4x2¼ inches.

MATERIALS *for each gift tag*

FABRIC
5x4-inch piece of 14-count white perforated paper
FLOSS
Cotton embroidery floss in colors listed in key
SUPPLIES
Needle; pencil
17-inch piece of red rattail cord
7½-inch piece of jute twine

INSTRUCTIONS

Find center of chart and center of perforated paper; begin stitching there. Use two plies of floss to work cross-stitches and one ply to work French knots and backstitches. Using pencil, draw stocking outline around stitched area as indicated on chart; cut out one square beyond markings.

Glue cord around stocking, starting at top right edge. Fold excess cord into a loop; glue end to back. Tie a small jute bow onto cord at stocking top.

★HOLLY JOLLY TREE SKIRT

As shown on pages 10–11.

MATERIALS

FABRIC
Purchased 26-inch-diameter jute tree skirt
THREADS
3-ply DMC Floralia wool in colors listed in key on page 22
Three additional skeins of green (DMC 7609) wool
One additional skein each of dark red (DMC 7107) and medium red (DMC 7566) wool
#8 metallic braid in color listed in key on page 22
SUPPLIES
Tapestry needle
1 yard of ⅞-inch-wide green satin ribbon
4½ yards of 1½-inch-wide red and gold satin ribbon
4½ yards of 2¼-inch-wide green satin ribbon
Button thread; sewing thread

INSTRUCTIONS

Find edge of inside skirt circle that is opposite opening; begin stitching top of center holly motif 2½ inches in from edge.

Use two strands of yarn (or 12 plies of cotton embroidery floss) to work cross-stitches over two threads of fabric. Use one strand of braid to work backstitches.

Press ends of narrow green ribbon under ¼ inch. Press in half lengthwise, wrong sides facing.

Pin green ribbon to straight edges and the inner circle of skirt, aligning ribbon fold with edge of skirt. Topstitch close to edge of ribbon.

For ruffle, press ends of ribbons under ¼ inch. Center and lay red ribbon atop green ribbon; pin.

Lay button thread ¼ inch from one edge of red ribbon. Use sewing thread to zigzag over button thread. Pull button thread to gather ribbons.

Pin gathered ribbons around skirt diameter; adjust gathers and topstitch ribbons in place.

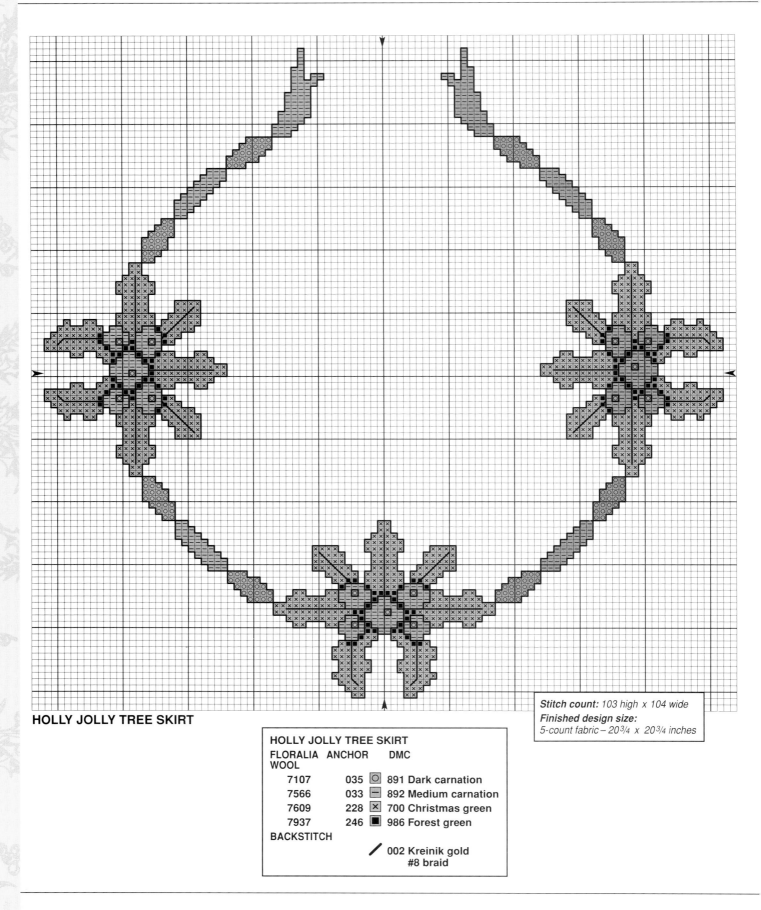

HOLLY JOLLY TREE SKIRT

Stitch count: 103 high x 104 wide
Finished design size:
5-count fabric – 20³⁄4 x 20³⁄4 inches

HOLLY JOLLY TREE SKIRT

FLORALIA WOOL	ANCHOR		DMC	
7107	035	⊙	891	Dark carnation
7566	033	–	892	Medium carnation
7609	228	✕	700	Christmas green
7937	246	■	986	Forest green

BACKSTITCH

╱ 002 Kreinik gold #8 braid

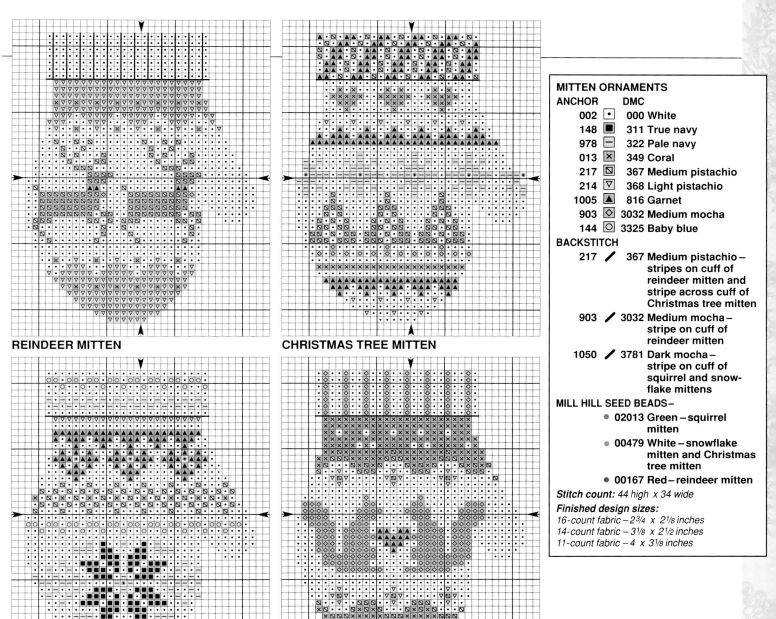

REINDEER MITTEN

CHRISTMAS TREE MITTEN

SNOWFLAKE MITTEN

SQUIRREL MITTEN

MITTEN ORNAMENTS			
ANCHOR		DMC	
002	·	000	White
148	■	311	True navy
978	–	322	Pale navy
013	✕	349	Coral
217	◩	367	Medium pistachio
214	▽	368	Light pistachio
1005	▲	816	Garnet
903	⊗	3032	Medium mocha
144	◎	3325	Baby blue

BACKSTITCH

217 ╱ 367 Medium pistachio – stripes on cuff of reindeer mitten and stripe across cuff of Christmas tree mitten

903 ╱ 3032 Medium mocha – stripe on cuff of reindeer mitten

1050 ╱ 3781 Dark mocha – stripe on cuff of squirrel and snowflake mittens

MILL HILL SEED BEADS –

● 02013 Green – squirrel mitten

● 00479 White – snowflake mitten and Christmas tree mitten

● 00167 Red – reindeer mitten

Stitch count: 44 high x 34 wide

Finished design sizes:
16-count fabric – 2³/₄ x 2¹/₈ inches
14-count fabric – 3¹/₈ x 2¹/₂ inches
11-count fabric – 4 x 3¹/₈ inches

★★SCANDINAVIAN MITTEN ORNAMENTS

As shown on page 12, finished mittens measure 2¹/₂ inches tall.

MATERIALS

For each ornament

FABRICS

6x6-inch piece of 32-count ivory Jobelan fabric
3¹/₂x3-inch piece of fleece
3¹/₂x3-inch piece of white felt

FLOSS

Cotton embroidery floss in colors listed in key

SUPPLIES

Needle; embroidery hoop
Seed beads in colors listed in key
¹/₂ yard of ¹/₈-inch-diameter red or green cord

INSTRUCTIONS

Tape or zigzag edges of fabric. Find center of chart and of fabric; begin stitching there. Use three plies of floss to work cross-stitches over two threads of fabric. Use one ply to work backstitches and to sew on beads.

Baste fleece to back of stitched piece, ¹/₄ inch beyond cross-stitching. Trim excess fabric ¹/₄ inch beyond basting. Using stitched piece as a pattern, cut a back from felt.

Sew front to back along basting lines, right sides together, leaving top open. Clip curves and turn.

Fold top edge over fleece; baste. Tack cord around sides of mitten; tie cord in bow at top to hang. Knot ends of cord.

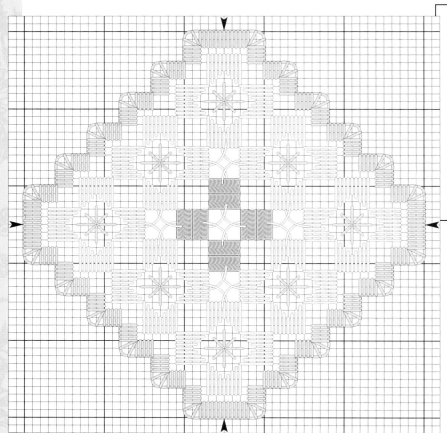

DIAMOND HARDANGER ORNAMENT

DIAMOND HARDANGER ORNAMENT
SATIN STITCH
(stitch in direction of symbol)
⬜ White #8 pearl cotton
BUTTONHOLE STITCH
⬜ White #8 pearl cotton
DIAMOND EYELET
✳ 032 Kreinik pearl #8 braid
NEEDLEWEAVING WITH WEB
▨ White #8 pearl cotton

Stitch count: 50 high x 50 wide
Finished design sizes:
25-count fabric – 4 x 4 inches
22-count fabric – 4½ x 4½ inches
28-count fabric – 3½ x 3½ inches

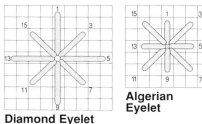

Diamond Eyelet Stitch

Algerian Eyelet

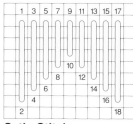

Satin Stitch

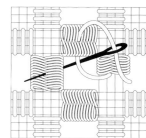

Web

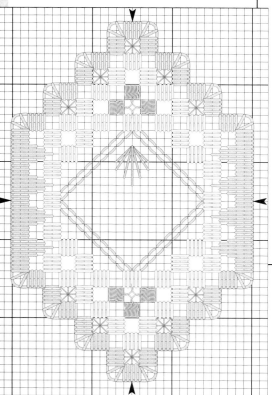

ANGEL HARDANGER ORNAMENT

ANGEL HARDANGER ORNAMENT
SATIN STITCH
(stitch in direction of symbol)
⬜ White #5 pearl cotton
BUTTONHOLE STITCH
⬜ White #5 pearl cotton
SMALL ALGERIAN EYELET
✳ White #8 pearl cotton
CABLE STITCH
▨ White #8 pearl cotton
STRAIGHT STITCH
⬜ White #5 pearl cotton
NEEDLEWEAVING WITH WEB
▨ White #8 pearl cotton

Stitch count: 46 high x 30 wide
Finished design sizes:
20-count fabric – 4⅝ x 3⅛ inches
22-count fabric – 4⅛ x 2⅞ inches
28-count fabric – 3¼ x 2¼ inches

Cable Stitch Step 1

Cable Stitch Step 2

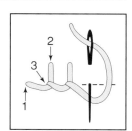

Buttonhole Stitch

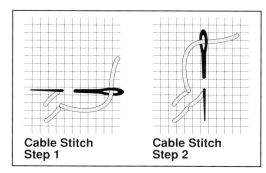

Needleweaving Step 1

Step 2

★★★★DIAMOND HARDANGER ORNAMENT

As shown on page 12.

MATERIALS

FABRIC
6x6-inch piece of 25-count white
   Lugana fabric
THREADS
#8 white pearl cotton
#8 braid in color listed in key
SUPPLIES
Needle
Embroidery hoop
Spray starch

INSTRUCTIONS

Tape or zigzag edges of fabric. Find top row of satin stitches on chart and vertical center of fabric. Measure 1½ inches from top of fabric and four threads to left of vertical center; begin first satin stitch there. For all stitches, refer to diagrams, *opposite.*

Work satin, buttonhole, and needleweaving stitches using one strand of pearl cotton. Work eyelets using one strand of braid; give each stitch a gentle tug to open a hole.

Cut and remove threads, referring to the needleweaving Step 1 diagram. Thread needle with a 30-inch length of pearl cotton. Work needleweaving, referring to Step 2 diagram and continuing with the webs.

Trim fabric around outside edge of ornament, close to stitching. Thread an 8-inch length of pearl cotton through top of ornament; knot ends. Lightly spray back of stitchery with starch; press using white press cloth.

★★★★ANGEL HARDANGER ORNAMENT

As shown on page 12.

MATERIALS

FABRIC
6x6-inch piece of 20-count white and
   silver Valerie fabric
THREADS
#8 and #5 white pearl cotton
SUPPLIES
Needle; embroidery hoop
Silver angel charm; spray starch

INSTRUCTIONS

Tape or zigzag edges of fabric. Find top row of satin stitches on chart and vertical center of fabric. Measure 1½ inches from top of fabric and two threads to left of fabric center; begin first satin stitch there.

Work all stitches referring to diagrams, *opposite.* Use one strand of #5 pearl cotton for satin, buttonhole, and eyelet stitches; use one strand #8 pearl cotton for all other stitches. For eyelets, give each stitch a gentle tug to open a small hole.

Cut and remove threads, referring to needleweaving Step 1 diagram. Thread a needle with a 30-inch length of #8 pearl cotton. Work needleweaving, referring to the Step 2 diagram and continuing with webs.

Trim fabric around the outside edge of ornament close to stitching. Lightly spray back of stitchery with starch; press using white press cloth.

Sew charm at bottom of longest straight stitch using #8 pearl cotton.

Thread an 8-inch length of #8 pearl cotton through top of ornament for hanger; knot ends together.

★★CELESTIAL ORNAMENTS

As shown on page 13.

MATERIALS *for each ornament*
FABRIC
6x6-inch piece of 14-count clear
   perforated plastic
THREADS
Cotton embroidery floss and #8 braid in
   colors listed in key on page 26
SUPPLIES
Needle

INSTRUCTIONS

Find center of chart and of plastic; begin stitching there. Use three plies of floss or one strand of braid to work cross-stitches. Work backstitches using one ply of floss.

Trim plastic one square beyond stitched area as indicated by dotted line on chart. Whipstitch edges of ornaments using one strand of gold braid. Thread an 8-inch length of braid through top for hanger; knot ends together.

★★SUN ROBE

As shown on page 13.

MATERIALS
FABRICS
6x6-inch piece of 28-count white
   Jobelan fabric
Purchased robe
THREADS
Cotton embroidery floss and
   #8 braid in colors listed in key on
   page 26
SUPPLIES
Needle; embroidery hoop; sewing thread

INSTRUCTIONS

Tape or zigzag edges of fabric. Find center of chart and of fabric; begin stitching there. Use three plies of floss or one strand of braid to work cross-stitches over two threads of fabric. Work backstitches using one ply of floss. Press finished stitchery.

Trim fabric ½ inch beyond stitched area; press raw edges to back. Position motif as desired; hand-sew to garment.

★MOON SLEEPER

As shown on page 13.

MATERIALS
FABRICS
Purchased white infant sleeper
8x8-inch piece of 14-count waste
   canvas; 5x5-inch piece of lightweight
   fusible interfacing (optional)
FLOSS
Cotton embroidery floss in colors listed
   in key on page 26
SUPPLIES
Basting thread; needle; ruler; tweezers

INSTRUCTIONS

Pre-wash the baby sleeper. Allow the sleeper to dry thoroughly.

Tape or zigzag the edges of the waste canvas to prevent fraying. Baste the waste canvas to the right side of the baby sleeper with the top edge of the waste canvas 3 inches below the shoulder seam.

Find the center of the chart and the center of the waste canvas; begin stitching there.

Use three plies of floss to work cross-stitches. Use one ply of floss to work backstitches.

Remove basting threads. Trim the waste canvas close to the stitching.

Wet waste canvas. Using tweezers, gently pull individual canvas threads from under the cross-stitches.

Fuse the lightweight interfacing over the cross-stitched motif on the inside of the moon baby sleeper following the instructions provided by the manufacturer.

CELESTIAL TREE ORNAMENTS

ANCHOR		DMC	
403	■	310	Black
150	●	336	Navy
	✕	002	Kreinik gold #8 braid
	I	021	Kreinik copper #8 braid
	–	022	Kreinik brown #8 braid
	•	032	Kreinik pearl #8 braid
	△	221	Kreinik antique gold #8 braid

BACKSTITCH
403	╱	310	Black

Stitch count: 43 high x 43 wide
Finished design size:
14-count fabric – 3¼ x 3¼ inches

SUN ROBE

ANCHOR		DMC	
403	■	310	Black
150	●	336	Navy
	△	021	Kreinik copper #8 braid
	•	032	Kreinik pearl #8 braid
	✕	221	Kreinik antique gold #8 braid

BACKSTITCH
403	╱	310	Black

Stitch count: 43 high x 43 wide
Finished design size:
14-count fabric – 3¼ x 3¼ inches

MOON BABY SLEEPER

ANCHOR		DMC	
002	•	000	White
150	●	336	Navy
381	–	938	Coffee brown
887	✕	3046	Yellow beige
1008	I	3773	Rose beige

BACKSTITCH
403	╱	310	Black

Stitch count: 43 high x 43 wide
Finished design size:
14-count fabric – 3¼ x 3¼ inches

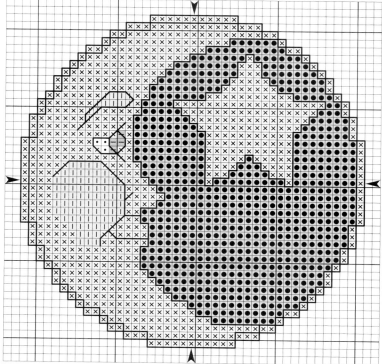

MOON

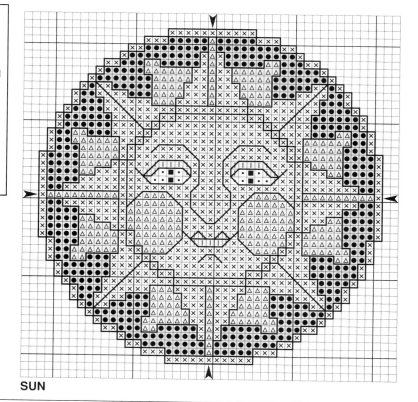

SUN

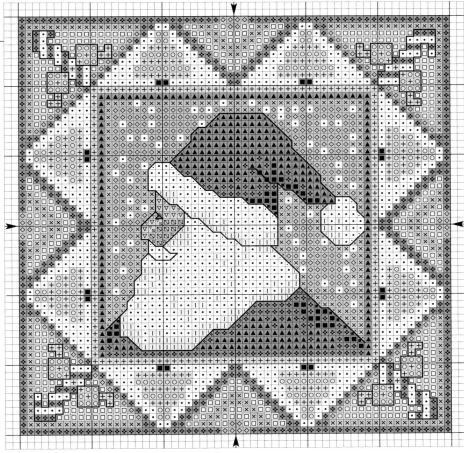

SANTA ORNAMENT AND SHIRT

ANCHOR		DMC	
002	⊡	000	White
9046	▲	321	Christmas red
227	⊞	701	Christmas green
256	⊙	704	Chartreuse
305	☐	725	Topaz
1021	▽	761	Salmon
234	⊟	762	Pearl gray
131	✕	798	Delft blue
045	■	814	Dark garnet
043	✛	815	Medium garnet
052	⊠	899	Rose
433	◇	996	Electric blue

BACKSTITCH

403	╱	310	Black – all stitches

Stitch count: 60 high x 60 wide

Finished design sizes:
14-count fabric – 4¼ x 4¼ inches
10-count fabric – 6 x 6 inches
6½-count fabric – 9¼ x 9¼ inches

SANTA ORNAMENT AND SHIRT

★★SANTA ORNAMENT

As shown on page 14, finished ornament measures 4¾x4¾ inches.

MATERIALS

FABRICS
8x8-inch piece of 28-count white Jubilee; 4¾x4¾-inch piece of felt

FLOSS
Cotton embroidery floss in colors listed in key

SUPPLIES
Needle; embroidery hoop; crafts glue
4¾x4¾-inch self-stick mounting board with foam
1 yard of ⅜-inch-wide black leather lacing

INSTRUCTIONS

Tape or zigzag edges of fabric. Find center of chart and center of fabric; begin stitching there. Use three plies of floss to work cross-stitches over two threads of fabric. Work backstitches using one ply.

Peel protective paper from back of mounting board. Center foam side on back of stitchery; press to stick. Trim fabric ½ inch beyond edge of board. Fold fabric edges to back; glue, mitering the corners. Beginning at the bottom center of ornament, glue lacing around edge; trim excess. Glue ends of remaining lacing to back at top, 1 inch from sides; tie loop into a knot at top. Glue felt to back.

★★SANTA SHIRT

As shown on page 14.

MATERIALS

FABRICS
Purchased green sweatshirt
9x9-inch piece of 10-count waste canvas
7x7-inch piece of lightweight fusible interfacing

FLOSS
Cotton embroidery floss in colors listed in key

SUPPLIES
Basting thread; needle
Tweezers; ruler

INSTRUCTIONS

Pre-wash sweatshirt. Allow shirt to dry thoroughly.

Tape or zigzag the edges of the waste canvas to prevent fraying. Baste waste canvas to the left side of the shirt front with center of top edge of the waste canvas 2½ inches below the center of the shoulder seam.

Find the center of the chart and the center of the waste canvas; begin stitching there.

Use four plies of floss to work cross-stitches, omitting the outer border as on the chart and the blue background behind the Santa portion of the design. Use two plies of floss to work the backstitches.

Remove the basting threads. Trim the waste canvas close to the stitching; wet the waste canvas.

Use tweezers to pull the individual waste canvas threads from under the cross-stitches.

Fuse the lightweight interfacing over the stitched area on the inside of the sweatshirt following the manufacturer's instructions.

27

Welcoming Wreaths

Greet your guests during this joyous season with a heartwarming holiday wreath. Within this chapter you'll discover a dazzling collection of festive wreath designs to brighten your front door as well as every nook and cranny of your holiday home. Inspired by the symbols of the season, our designs range from fun and whimsical to elegant and gracious and will surely be loved by all.

Sweet Candy Train

The stitched treats on this merry yuletide wreath will bring smiles to the young and young at heart. Stitched on perforated plastic, these candy train cars are created entirely in half cross-stitches to work up quickly for playful holiday decorating. For the festive centerpiece, fill jars with real confections and surround them with evergreens, garland, and stitched peppermints and train cars. Instructions and charts begin on page 35.

DESIGNER: RUTH SCHMUFF
PHOTOGRAPHERS: OPPOSITE, SCOTT LITTLE; ABOVE, HOPKINS ASSOCIATES

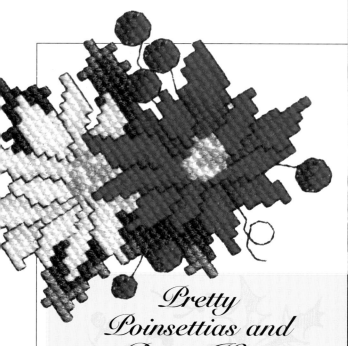

Pretty Poinsettias and Brass Horn

A brass horn embellished with red and white poinsettias and bright red berries takes center stage in this spectacular wreath-shaped design. Display your completed stitchery in a rich wooden petite serving tray or stitch just part of the design and insert it into a handsome holiday coaster. A single poinsettia motif stitched on 28-count white Brittney fabric makes elegant dinner napkins. The entire hostess set will add that extra-special touch to your holiday entertaining. Instructions and charts begin on page 36.

DESIGNER: CAROLE RODGERS
PHOTOGRAPHER: SCOTT LITTLE

Merry Bear Wreath and Stacking Blocks

Two favorite childhood toys are combined in this adorable Christmas wreath design—alphabet blocks and the best-loved toy of all, a huggable teddy bear. The cheerful design is even more special when framed with an eight-sided mat. You can also create a three-dimensional version of the design by stitching the letters on perforated paper and attaching them to wooden blocks painted in crayon-bright colors. Instructions and chart begin on page 37.

DESIGNER: CAROLE RODGERS ● PHOTOGRAPHER: HOPKINS ASSOCIATES

Rat-a-tat Toy Soldier

Surrounded by metallic bows and tiny silver drums, our dashing toy soldier stands at attention on this enchanting holiday wreath. This proud character is stitched on perforated plastic and is accented with beaded epaulets and a striking black hat made of fun-to-do turkey work.
Instructions and chart are on page 39.

DESIGNER: VIRGINIA DOUGLAS ● PHOTOGRAPHER: HOPKINS ASSOCIATES

Welcoming Wreaths

Della Robbia Wreath

Inspired by the traditional fruit Christmas wreaths that have graced the doorways of elegant homes since Colonial times, this gorgeous design features a ring of colorful oranges, pears, persimmons, and grapes. The rich wreath motif is worked entirely of whole stitches on 28-count Quaker cloth and will provide a delightful welcome for guests long after the Christmas ornaments are packed away. Instructions and chart are on pages 40–41.

DESIGNER: JIM WILLIAMS ● PHOTOGRAPHER: HOPKINS ASSOCIATES

CANDY TRAIN WREATH AND CENTERPIECE

As shown on pages 28–29.

MATERIALS

FABRIC *for each train car*
6x7-inch piece of 14-count clear perforated plastic
FABRIC *for each peppermint*
2x2-inch piece of 14-count clear perforated plastic
THREADS
Cotton embroidery floss and #16 braid in colors listed in key
SUPPLIES
Needle; wreath or greens; 1½ yards 2-inch-wide pastel ribbon, floral wire, and small pink and gold round ornaments or red bead garland

INSTRUCTIONS

Find center of chart and of plastic; begin stitching there. Use six plies of floss or one strand of braid to work *half cross-stitches* in direction indicated on key. *All stitches are half cross-stitches.*

Trim plastic one square beyond stitching as indicated on chart. Whipstitch edges using six plies white floss. For centerpiece candies, stitch wheel portions from engine chart, *right.*

For wreath, tie bow in center of ribbon; wire to top. Attach cars and round ornaments evenly spaced. For centerpiece, lay stitchery on greens, adding bead garland as desired.

ENGINE and CAR stitch count: 48 high x 49 wide
ENGINE and CAR finished design sizes:
14-count fabric – 3⅜ x 3½ inches
8½-count fabric – 5⅝ x 5¾ inches
6½-count fabric – 7⅜ x 7½ inches

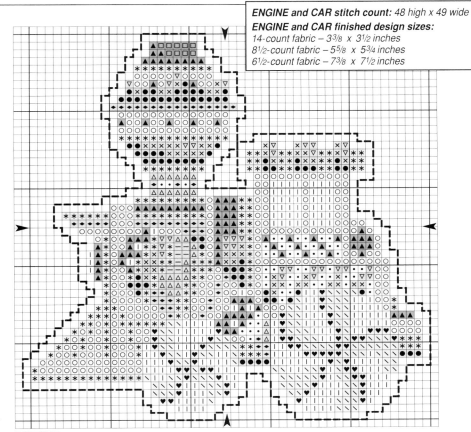

ENGINE

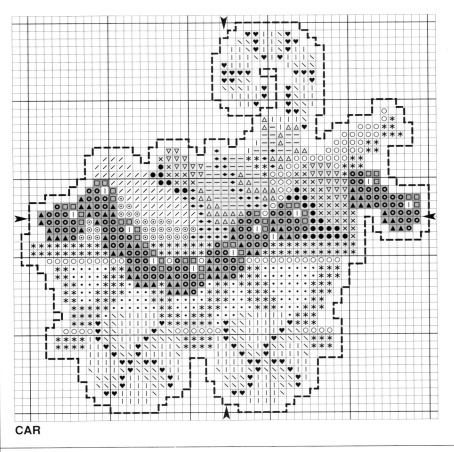

CAR

CANDY TRAIN HALF CROSS-STITCHES (╱)			
ANCHOR			**DMC**
002	·		000 White
110	✦		208 Dark lavender
109	△		209 Medium lavender
342	—		211 Pale lavender
9046	◎		321 Christmas red
046	□		666 Red
923	●		699 Dark Christmas green
227	✕		701 True Christmas green
238	▽		703 Chartreuse
1005	▲		816 Garnet
	╱		001 Kreinik silver #16 braid
	✳		002 Kreinik gold #16 braid
	⊙		011HL Kreinik gunmetal #16 braid
	♥		024 Kreinik fuchsia #16 braid
	│		032 Kreinik pearl #16 braid
	╲		092 Kreinik star pink #16 braid
	○		102HL Kreinik Vatican #16 braid

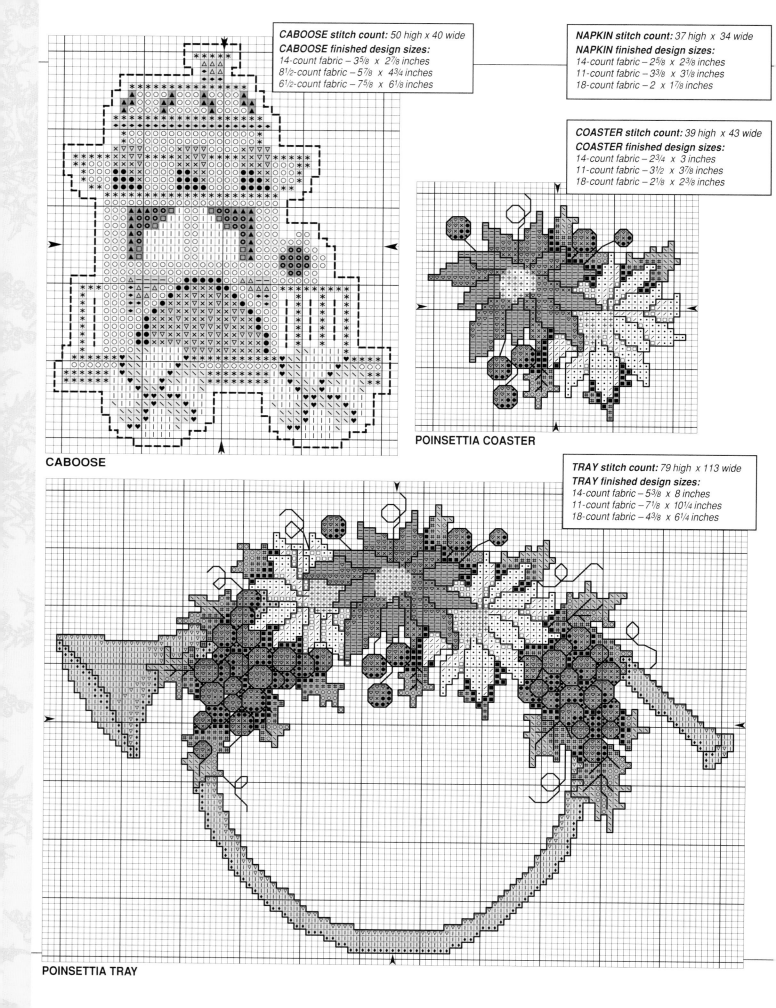

CABOOSE stitch count: *50 high x 40 wide*
CABOOSE finished design sizes:
14-count fabric – 3⅝ x 2⅞ inches
8½-count fabric – 5⅞ x 4¾ inches
6½-count fabric – 7⅝ x 6⅛ inches

NAPKIN stitch count: *37 high x 34 wide*
NAPKIN finished design sizes:
14-count fabric – 2⅝ x 2⅜ inches
11-count fabric – 3⅜ x 3⅛ inches
18-count fabric – 2 x 1⅞ inches

COASTER stitch count: *39 high x 43 wide*
COASTER finished design sizes:
14-count fabric – 2¾ x 3 inches
11-count fabric – 3½ x 3⅞ inches
18-count fabric – 2⅛ x 2⅜ inches

CABOOSE

POINSETTIA COASTER

TRAY stitch count: *79 high x 113 wide*
TRAY finished design sizes:
14-count fabric – 5⅜ x 8 inches
11-count fabric – 7⅛ x 10¼ inches
18-count fabric – 4⅜ x 6¼ inches

POINSETTIA TRAY

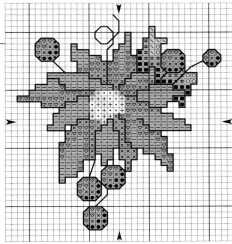

POINSETTIA NAPKIN

POINSETTIA HOSTESS SET		
ANCHOR		DMC
002	·	000 White
218	#	319 Dark pistachio
215	⊠	320 True pistachio
9046	–	321 True Christmas red
217	○	367 Medium pistachio
1005	♡	498 Dark Christmas red
683	■	500 Blue green
926	╱	712 Cream
279	+	734 Olive
310	◆	780 Deep topaz
308	▽	782 Medium topaz
307	⊡	783 Christmas gold
043	✕	815 Medium garnet
390	□	822 Beige gray
897	●	902 Deep garnet
BACKSTITCH		
381	╱	938 Coffee brown– all stitches

★★POINSETTIA TRAY

As shown on page 31.

MATERIALS
FABRICS
11x13-inch piece of 28-count white Brittney fabric
9x12-inch piece of fleece
FLOSS
Cotton embroidery floss in colors listed in key
SUPPLIES
Embroidery hoop; needle
Purchased 9x12-inch wood tray
Red mat; spray adhesive; masking tape

INSTRUCTIONS
Tape or zigzag the edges of fabric. Find center of chart and of fabric; begin stitching there. Use three plies of floss to work cross-stitches over two threads of fabric. Work back-stitches using one ply. Press finished stitchery from the back; set aside.

Cut fleece the same size as mounting board from tray. Spray board lightly with adhesive and position fleece on top. Center design on board; tape edges to back. Insert red mat; assemble tray following manufacturer's instructions.

★★POINSETTIA COASTER

As shown on page 31.

MATERIALS
FABRICS
8x8-inch piece of 28-count white Brittney fabric
6x6-inch piece of fleece
FLOSS
Cotton embroidery floss in colors listed in key
SUPPLIES
Purchased 5-inch-diameter wood coaster

INSTRUCTIONS
Tape or zigzag edges of fabric to prevent fraying. Find center of chart and of fabric; begin stitching there. Use three plies of floss to work cross-stitches over two threads of fabric. Work backstitches using one ply.

Press finished stitchery. Insert fabric into coaster following the manufacturer's instructions.

★★POINSETTIA NAPKIN

As shown on page 30.

MATERIALS *for each napkin*
FABRIC
16¼x16¼-inch piece of 28-count white Brittney fabric
FLOSS
Cotton embroidery floss in colors listed in key; one additional skein DMC 498
SUPPLIES
Needle; embroidery hoop
White sewing thread; gold metallic thread; 1⅛ yards of ½-inch-wide white picot-edged lace

INSTRUCTIONS
Zigzag the fabric edges. Measure 2½ inches from edges at lower left corner; begin stitching the poinsettia center there.

Use three plies of floss to work cross-stitches over two threads of fabric. Work backstitches using one ply. Press the stitchery from the back.

Fold zigzagged edges under ¼ inch, mitering corners; press. Pin lace to the wrong side of hem; topstitch. Lay red floss (DMC 498) around the perimeter, ¼ inch from edge. Using gold metallic thread, zigzag over red floss.

★STACKING BLOCKS

As shown on page 32.

MATERIALS
FABRIC
Fourteen 3x3-inch pieces of 14-count brown perforated paper
FLOSS
Cotton embroidery floss in colors listed in key on page 38
SUPPLIES
Needle
Fourteen 2½-inch wooden blocks
Red, green, blue, orange, and purple acrylic paints; paintbrush
56 assorted buttons
Crafts glue; wood glue

INSTRUCTIONS
For each block, find center of letter block on chart and of perforated paper; begin stitching there. Use two plies of floss to work cross-stitches. Work backstitches using one ply.

Work entire block border for each of the blocks, omitting portions of main design as necessary and filling in to complete full border. Trim paper one square beyond the stitched area.

Paint blocks using acrylic paint as follows; three red blocks, three blue blocks, two orange blocks, three green blocks, and three purple blocks. Allow to dry. Referring to photograph, glue each stitched piece to a side of a wood block; glue buttons to the corners.

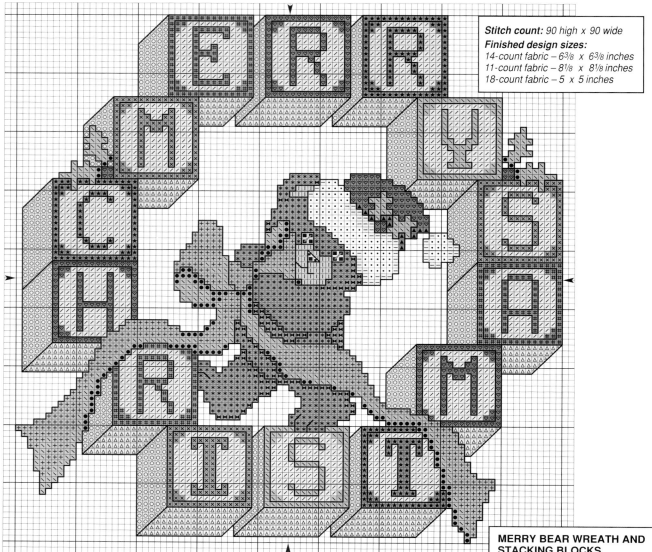

Stitch count: 90 high x 90 wide
Finished design sizes:
14-count fabric – 6³⁄₈ x 6³⁄₈ inches
11-count fabric – 8¹⁄₈ x 8¹⁄₈ inches
18-count fabric – 5 x 5 inches

MERRY BEAR WREATH AND STACKING BLOCKS

★MERRY BEAR WREATH

As shown on page 32 and on cover.

MATERIALS

FABRIC
13x13-inch piece of 14-count white Aida cloth

FLOSS
Cotton embroidery floss in colors listed in key

SUPPLIES
Needle
Embroidery hoop
Mat
Frame

INSTRUCTIONS

Tape or zigzag edges of fabric to prevent fraying. Find center of chart and of fabric; begin stitching there.

Use three plies of floss to work cross-stitches. Work straight stitches using two plies of floss. Work back-stitches using one ply of floss.

Press finished stitchery from the back and frame as desired.

Note: As photographed on page 32, this wreath design is framed with an eight-sided mat and square frame. On the cover, the design was framed in a fabric-covered, eight-sided mat with an eight-sided frame.

MERRY BEAR WREATH AND STACKING BLOCKS		
ANCHOR	DMC	
002	000	White
403	310	Black
9046	321	Christmas red
102	550	Violet
334	606	Orange red
923	699	Dark Christmas green
228	700	Medium Christmas green
234	762	Pearl gray
133	796	Royal blue
1005	816	Garnet
380	838	Deep beige brown
360	839	Dark beige brown
378	841	True beige brown
1044	895	Hunter green
888	3045	Dark yellow beige
887	3046	Medium yellow beige
886	3047	Light yellow beige
STRAIGHT STITCH		
002	000	White – eye highlights
BACKSTITCH		
403	310	Black – facial and toe features
381	938	Coffee brown – all remaining stitches

★★RAT-A-TAT TOY SOLDIER WREATH

As shown on page 33.

MATERIALS *for one soldier*

FABRIC
7x3-inch piece of 14-count clear
perforated plastic

THREADS
Cotton embroidery floss in colors listed
in key
#8 braid in color listed in key

SUPPLIES
Needle; seed beads
Floral wire; pine branch
Six 1-inch-diameter silver drum
ornaments
1 yard of ⅛-inch-wide gold
metallic ribbon
1 yard of ⅛-inch-wide silver
metallic ribbon
2½ yards of ⅞-inch-wide burgundy and
gold wire-edged ribbon
25 inches of ¼-inch-wide gold ribbon
4-inch-wide piece of cardboard

INSTRUCTIONS

Find the center of chart and the
center of perforated plastic; begin
stitching there.

Use two plies of floss or one strand
of braid to work cross-stitches. Work
backstitches using one ply of floss.

Use four plies of floss for turkey
work, referring to diagrams, *right.*
Clip turkey work to ⅛ inch.

Trim plastic one square beyond
stitched area as indicated by dotted
line on chart. Sew bead rows to
jacket shoulders using two plies of
white floss.

For bead fringe, bring needle from
the back through far left hole in plastic under shoulder bead rows. Slip
three beads on the needle. Slip fourth
bead on the needle; insert needle back
through the first three beads, exiting
at back of soldier. Repeat until there
are five bead strings below each
shoulder epaulet.

Using floral wire, attach soldier to
the center of the pine branch. Use
wire to secure drums around soldier.

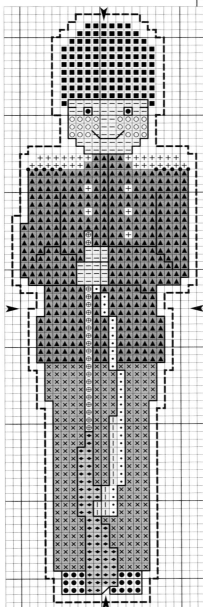

TOY SOLDIER WREATH

Cut the ⅛-inch-wide gold and
silver ribbons into 6-inch lengths.
Tie the ribbon pieces into bows;
randomly wire bows around soldier.

Cut a 25-inch piece from burgundy
ribbon; set aside. Wrap the remaining
ribbon around the 4-inch piece of
cardboard; carefully remove, holding
ribbons together in the center. Tie the
25-inch lengths of burgundy and gold
ribbons around the center of the bow;
knot in back. Use floral wire to attach
bow to top of wreath, winding ribbon
ends through pine branch.

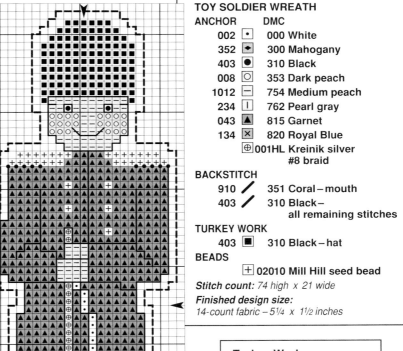

TOY SOLDIER WREATH

ANCHOR		DMC	
002	⊡	000	White
352	◆	300	Mahogany
403	●	310	Black
008	○	353	Dark peach
1012	⊟	754	Medium peach
234	⊺	762	Pearl gray
043	▲	815	Garnet
134	⊠	820	Royal Blue
	⊕	001HL	Kreinik silver #8 braid

BACKSTITCH

910	╱	351	Coral – mouth
403	╱	310	Black – all remaining stitches

TURKEY WORK

403	▪	310	Black – hat

BEADS

	⊞	02010	Mill Hill seed bead

Stitch count: 74 high x 21 wide
Finished design size:
14-count fabric – 5¼ x 1½ inches

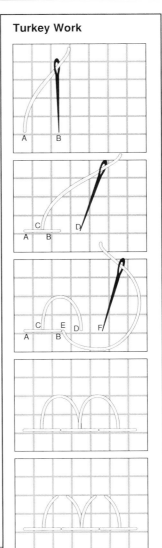

Turkey Work

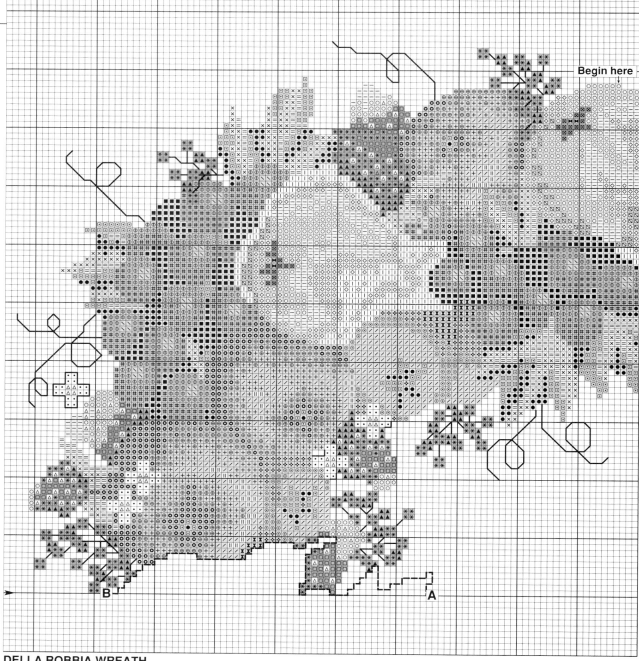

Begin here

DELLA ROBBIA WREATH

★★★DELLA ROBBIA WREATH
As shown on page 34.

MATERIALS
FABRIC
22x22-inch piece of 28-count country
   Quaker cloth
FLOSS
Cotton embroidery floss in colors listed
   in key
One additional skein of each of the
   following DMC colors: 327, 352, 553,
   722, 817, 834, 900, 946, and 971

SUPPLIES
Basting thread
Embroidery hoop
Needle
Desired mat and frame

INSTRUCTIONS
Tape or zigzag the edges of the
fabric to prevent fraying. Measure
3½ inches down from the top center
of fabric; start stitching top pear as
indicated by the arrow on the chart.

Use three plies of floss to work all
cross-stitches over two threads of

the fabric. Work backstitches using
two plies of floss. Stitch the entire
chart to complete the upper half of
the wreath design.

Rotate the fabric 180° when the
top half of the wreath design is completely stitched. Align points A and B
as indicated by the dotted lines on
the chart.

Stitch the second half of the wreath
design in the same manner, working
cross-stitches over two threads of
fabric. Press the finished stitchery
from the back and frame as desired.

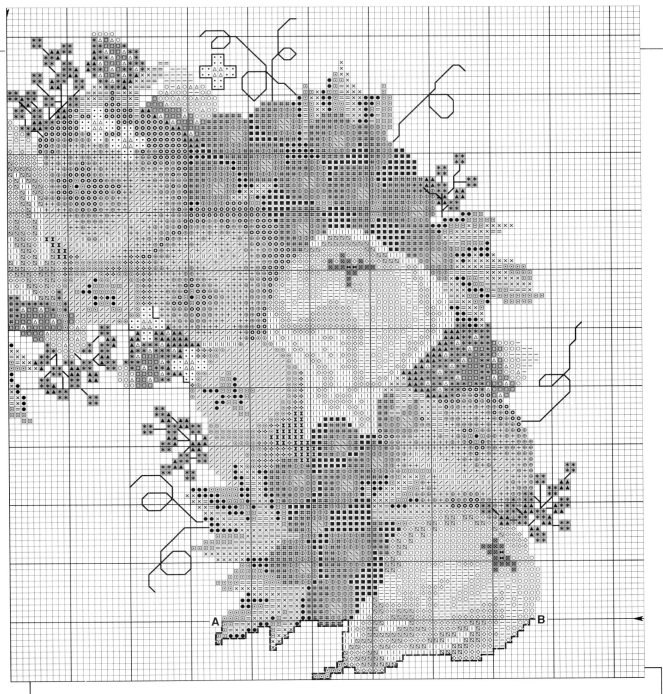

DELLA ROBBIA WREATH

ANCHOR		DMC		ANCHOR		DMC		ANCHOR		DMC	
002	•	000 White		279	◳	734 Olive		316	+	971 Pumpkin	
100	⊞	327 Deep antique violet		302	△	743 Yellow		298	‖	972 Canary	
011	▣	350 Medium coral		259	│	772 Loden		355	⊠	975 Golden brown	
009	○	352 Pale coral		359	◄	801 Coffee brown		870	◲	3042 Light antique violet	
008	−	353 Peach		043	▲	815 Garnet					
267	▣	470 Medium avocado		013	✳	817 Deep coral		**BACKSTITCH**			
266	✕	471 Light avocado		127	■	823 Navy		359	╱	801 Coffee brown –	
253	═	472 Pale avocado		945	◇	834 Bronze				grape tendrils,	
098	⏀	553 Violet		333	◉	900 Dark burnt orange				currant stems	
326	✤	720 Dark bittersweet		1014	✖	919 Red copper					
324	⊙	721 Medium bittersweet		268	●	937 Pine green					
323	╱	722 Light bittersweet		332	⊕	946 Medium burnt orange					

Stitch count: 206 high x 206 wide

Finished design sizes:
14-count fabric – 14³/₄ x 14³/₄ inches
16-count fabric – 12⁷/₈ x 12⁷/₈ inches
18-count fabric – 11¹/₂ x 11¹/₂ inches

Stockings for Santa

*O*n Christmas morning, children all over the world race to their stockings to discover the treats Santa has left for them. That wonderful tradition will become even more special with the select group of stocking designs found here and on the following pages. As a bonus, you'll find that small portions from two of the designs make fun-to-stitch ornaments, perfect for a miniature or a full-size tree.

Cookie Jar Stocking and Ornaments

Worked on 25-count navy Lugana fabric, this whimsical design features merry mice preparing a plate of cookies for Santa. Tiny seed beads and jingle bells add clever detail as the backstitches add definition to the playful characters. For those with longer names, we've also provided a condensed version of the alphabet. To make especially sweet tree ornaments, stitch a dozen chocolate chip cookies using the motif from the bottom of the stocking. Instructions and charts begin on page 47.

DESIGNER: LORRI BIRMINGHAM ● PHOTOGRAPHER: HOPKINS ASSOCIATES

Stockings for Santa

Southwestern Stocking and Ornaments

We've corralled the best of the Southwest in these eye-catching designs. Easily cross-stitched on red Aida cloth, the stocking design is then machine-quilted using gold metallic sewing thread. The colorful stocking is highlighted with soft chamois fringes that are trimmed with red and green barrel beads. Stitch up several of the geometric shapes in desired color combinations to use as ornaments for a striking Southwestern Christmas tree. Complete instructions and charts begin on page 50.

DESIGNER: JIM WILLIAMS ● PHOTOGRAPHER: HOPKINS ASSOCIATES

Scandinavian Stocking

Worked on 28-count amaretto Jubilee fabric, the delicate shading on this charming stocking gives the cuff, toe, and heel the look of a real knit stocking. The rosy-cheeked children are worked in rich hues—the subtle color changes and French knots adding to the splendid details of their frilly ethnic costumes. Complete instructions and chart begin on page 54.

DESIGNER: MAUREEN MCDOUGALL
PHOTOGRAPHER: HOPKINS ASSOCIATES

Jester Stocking

Running stitches of red and gold threads form a dainty plaid background for the shining cross-stitched jingle bells on our festive stocking. Finished with gold piping and a red cuff, this fun design is sure to bring smiles to kids of all ages. For the special finishing touch, real jingle bells are sewn to the points of the cuff and the stocking toe. Complete instructions and chart begin on page 56.

DESIGNER: JIM WILLIAMS
PHOTOGRAPHER: HOPKINS ASSOCIATES

46

Stockings for Santa

★★★COOKIE JAR STOCKING

As shown on page 42, finished stocking measures 18½ inches tall.

MATERIALS
FABRICS
22x16-inch piece of 25-count navy Lugana fabric
¾ yard of 45-inch-wide pastel stripe cotton fabric
20x15-inch piece of fusible fleece
FLOSS
Cotton embroidery floss in colors listed in key on pages 48–49
SUPPLIES
Needle; embroidery hoop
Graph paper
Erasable fabric marker
1⅓ yards of ¼-inch-diameter cording
Three ⅜-inch-diameter jingle bells
Red and black seed beads
2-inch-diameter gold jingle bell
Two 3½-inch-long red tassels
2 yards of ⅝-inch-diameter metallic gold and white cord

INSTRUCTIONS
Tape or zigzag edges of the Lugana fabric to prevent fraying. Find the center of the chart and the center of the fabric; begin stitching there.

Use three plies of floss to work cross-stitches over two threads of fabric. Work backstitches using one ply of floss.

For personalized name on cuff, refer to alphabet charts on pages 50–51. For names with more than five letters, use the condensed letters from chart on page 50. For names with five or less letters, use the letters from chart on page 51. The key for both alphabet charts is on page 48.

Chart the name on the graph paper, using the appropriate alphabet and separating each letter with two squares. Begin stitching the name so it is centered left to right and bottom row of stitches is 14 threads above the stitched lower border design.

Use the erasable fabric marker to draw an outline as indicated on chart.

Fuse the piece of fleece to the back of the Lugana cloth following the manufacturer's instructions.

Cut out the stocking ¼ inch beyond the marker line. Use the Lugana cloth stocking as a pattern to cut one back piece and two lining pieces from the cotton fabric.

Also from the cotton fabric, cut a 1½x5-inch hanging strip, two 4x24-inch bias ruffle strips, and two 1¼x24-inch bias piping strips. All of the measurements include ¼-inch seam allowances.

Sew the two short ends of the piping strips together. Center the cording lengthwise on the wrong side of the piping strip.

Fold the fabric around the cording with the raw edges together. Use a zipper foot to sew through both layers close to cording. Baste the piping around the sides of the stocking front with the raw edges even.

Sew the stocking front to the back with the right sides together, along basting, using ¼-inch seams. Leave the top edge open. Use sewing thread to attach the small jingle bells to the tips of the mouse caps, the black beads to the mouse eyes, and the red beads to the holly berries.

Press long edges of hanging strip under ¼ inch. Fold the strip in half lengthwise; topstitch. Fold the topstitched piece in half to form a loop. Tack the loop to the inside top right edge of the stocking.

Join the ends of ruffle strips together to form a continuous circle. Fold in half lengthwise.

Sew a gathering thread through both layers of the ruffle strip ¼ inch from the raw edges. Pull the threads to fit the top edge of the stocking with the raw edges even; adjust the gathers evenly. Sew the ruffle to the stocking top.

Sew the lining pieces together, right sides together, leaving the top open and an opening at bottom of foot; *do not* turn.

Slip the stocking inside the lining. Stitch the stocking to the lining at the top edges with right sides of the fabrics together; turn. Slip-stitch the stocking opening closed. Tuck the lining into the stocking. Press stocking carefully.

Sew the tassels to the top right corner of the stocking. Cut the metallic gold and white cord into two equal pieces. Insert the ends of both pieces of cord through the loop at the top of the 2-inch-diameter jingle bell. Tie the cord into a bow.

Tack the cord bow to the top right corner of the stocking. Tie knots in ends of cord.

★COOKIE JAR ORNAMENT

As shown on page 43, cookie ornaments measure 1½x1⅝ inches.

MATERIALS
for each ornament
FABRICS
3x3-inch piece of 14-count clear perforated plastic
3x3-inch piece of brown felt
FLOSS
Cotton embroidery floss in colors listed in key on pages 48–49
SUPPLIES
Needle
Crafts glue
12-inch piece of ⅛-inch-wide red and white polka-dot satin ribbon

INSTRUCTIONS
Find the center of the cookie motif below the mug on the stocking chart, *page 49,* and the center of the perforated plastic; begin stitching there.

Use three plies of floss to work cross-stitches. Use two plies of floss to work backstitches. Stitch as many of the cookie ornaments as desired.

Trim plastic one square beyond the stitched area. Use stitched piece as a pattern to cut a felt back.

Cut a 6-inch piece of ribbon. Fold ribbon in half to form a loop. Glue ends of ribbon to back of cookie.

Tie the remaining ribbon into a small bow. Glue the bow to the top right corner of the cookie. Glue the felt back to the cookie.

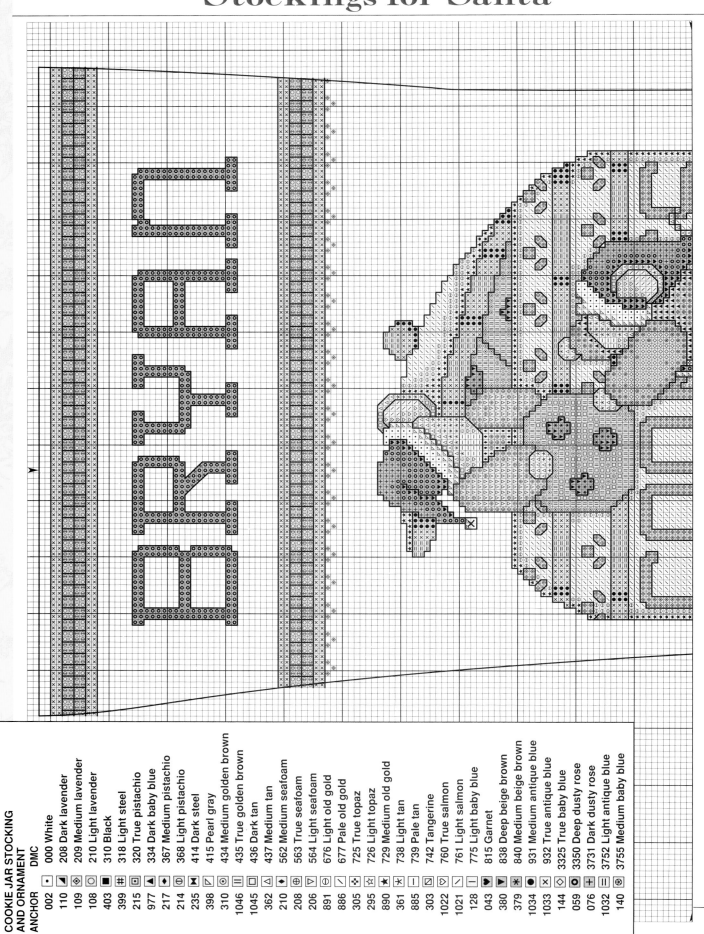

COOKIE JAR STOCKING AND ORNAMENT

ANCHOR		DMC
002	•	000 White
110	◢	208 Dark lavender
109	◈	209 Medium lavender
108	○	210 Light lavender
403	■	310 Black
399	#	318 Light steel
215	⊡	320 True pistachio
977	▲	334 Dark baby blue
217	◆	367 Medium pistachio
214	⦶	368 Light pistachio
235	⧓	414 Dark steel
398	◸	415 Pearl gray
310	⊙	434 Medium golden brown
1046	‖	435 True golden brown
1045	□	436 Dark tan
362	△	437 Medium tan
210	◆	562 Medium seafoam
208	⊕	563 True seafoam
206	▽	564 Light seafoam
891	⊖	676 Light old gold
886	/	677 Pale old gold
305	⁜	725 True topaz
295	☆	726 Light topaz
890	★	729 Medium old gold
361	✳	738 Light tan
885	−	739 Pale tan
303	⧅	742 Tangerine
1022	♡	760 True salmon
1021	\	761 Light salmon
128	|	775 Light baby blue
043	♥	815 Garnet
380	▼	838 Deep beige brown
379	✱	840 Medium beige brown
1034	●	931 Medium antique blue
1033	×	932 True antique blue
144	◇	3325 True baby blue
059	◉	3350 Deep dusty rose
076	+	3731 Dark dusty rose
1032	=	3752 Light antique blue
140	⊛	3755 Medium baby blue

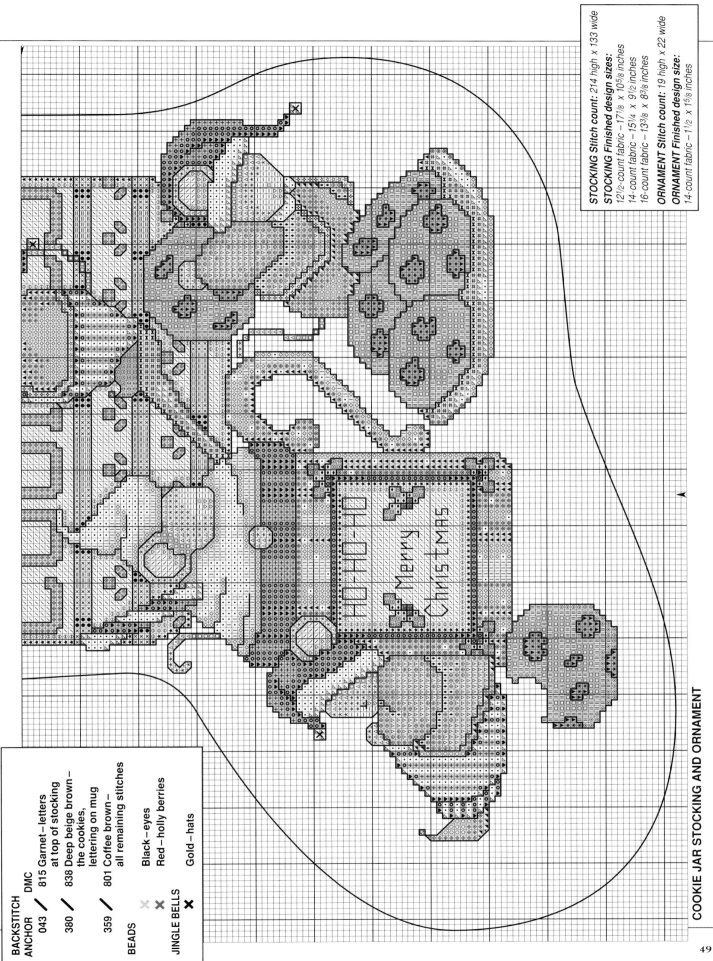

BACKSTITCH

ANCHOR		DMC	
043	/	815	Garnet – letters at top of stocking
380	/	838	Deep beige brown – the cookies, lettering on mug
359	/	801	Coffee brown – all remaining stitches

BEADS

✕ Black – eyes
✕ Red – holly berries

JINGLE BELLS

✕ Gold – hats

STOCKING Stitch count: 214 high x 133 wide
STOCKING Finished design sizes:
12½-count fabric – 17⅛ x 10⅝ inches
14-count fabric – 15¼ x 9½ inches
16-count fabric – 13⅜ x 8⅜ inches

ORNAMENT Stitch count: 19 high x 22 wide
ORNAMENT Finished design size:
14-count fabric – 1½ x 1⅝ inches

COOKIE JAR STOCKING AND ORNAMENT

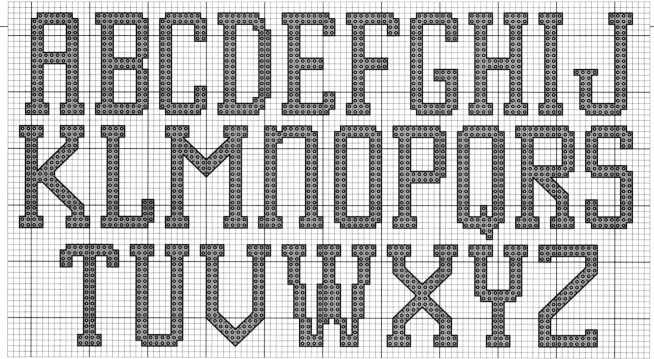

COOKIE JAR STOCKING ALPHABET – CONDENSED

★★SOUTHWESTERN STOCKING

As shown on page 44, finished stocking measures 16 inches tall.

MATERIALS
FABRICS
22x14-inch piece of 11-count Victorian red Aida cloth
½ yard of gold wool fabric
¾ yard of beige cotton fabric
18x12-inch piece of fusible fleece
3x10-inch piece of chamois leather
FLOSS
Cotton embroidery floss in colors listed in key on page 52
SUPPLIES
Needle; embroidery hoop
Erasable fabric marker
42-inch piece of purchased gold piping
17 red ¾-inch-long barrel beads
17 green ¾-inch-long barrel beads
1-inch-diameter copper bead or button
Gold metallic sewing thread

INSTRUCTIONS
Tape or zigzag the edges of Aida cloth to prevent fraying. Find center of chart and center of fabric; begin stitching there. Use three plies of floss to work cross-stitches.

Use the marker to draw an outline as indicated on chart. Fuse the fleece to back of Aida cloth.

Cut out stocking ¼ inch beyond marker line. Use Aida cloth stocking as a pattern to cut one back from gold wool and two lining pieces from cotton fabric. Also cut a 1½x5-inch strip from wool fabric.

Machine-quilt around shapes, as indicated by dotted lines on chart, using gold metallic thread. Baste piping around sides and foot of stocking front with raw edges even. Sew front to back with right sides facing, using ¼-inch seams. Leave top open.

Cut a 7½x3-inch strip from chamois. Make 2½-inch-long cuts spaced ¼ inch apart along length of strip. With edges even, sew chamois to stocking top.

Press long edges of wool strip under ¼ inch. Fold strip in half lengthwise; topstitch. Fold wool strip in half to form a loop. Tack loop to inside top right edge of stocking.

Sew lining pieces together, with right sides together, leaving top open and an opening at bottom of foot. *Do not* turn. Slip stocking inside lining. Stitch stocking to lining at top edges; turn. Slip-stitch the opening closed. Tuck the lining into the stocking and press carefully.

Fringe remaining chamois as before. Tack remaining chamois to center motif of stocking. Sew large bead over chamois. Slip barrel beads onto all chamois strips; knot the ends.

★★SOUTHWESTERN ORNAMENTS

As shown on page 44, ornaments including tassels are 6¼ inches tall.

MATERIALS
for each ornament
FABRICS
6x6-inch piece of 11-count Victorian red Aida cloth
¼x5-inch strip of chamois leather
2¼x2¼-inch piece of chamois leather
5x1-inch strip of chamois leather (optional)
FLOSS
Cotton embroidery floss in colors listed in key on page 52
SUPPLIES
Needle; embroidery hoop
1¾x1¾-inch piece of self-stick mounting board with foam
Four ¾-inch-long barrel beads (optional)
⅝-inch-diameter silver flat bead or button
Pinking shears; crafts glue

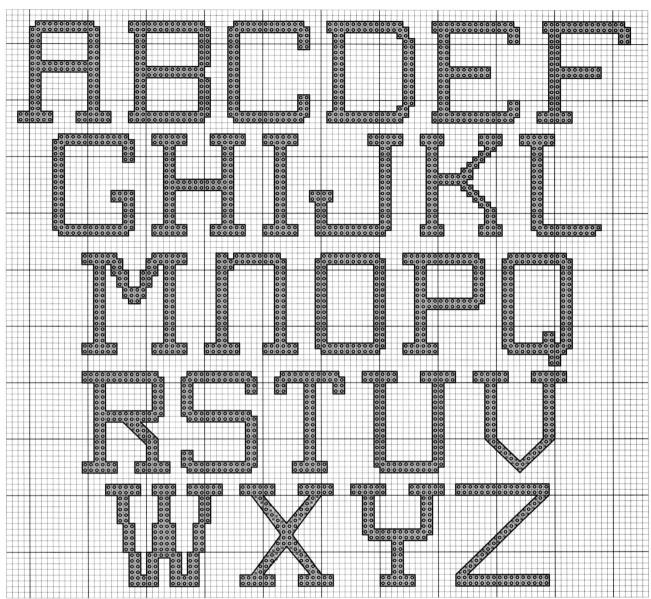

COOKIE JAR STOCKING ALPHABET – AS SHOWN

INSTRUCTIONS

Tape or zigzag edges of Aida cloth to prevent fraying. Find the center of chart and the center of fabric; begin stitching there. Use three plies of floss to work the cross-stitches as shown on the chart, *page 53*, or in desired color combinations.

Peel the protective paper from the mounting board. Position the stitched motif on back of the board; press to stick. Trim the fabric ½ inch beyond the mounting board. Fold the raw edges to the back, mitering the corners, and glue.

Cut four 1-yard lengths from desired floss colors. Combine the cut lengths into a single strand. Secure one end of the floss and twist; fold in half and allow to twist together.

For ornament with floss tassel, find center of twisted cord; place at one corner of ornament and glue with cord meeting at opposite corner. Cut an 8-inch length of floss. Wrap floss around both twisted cords where they meet. Glue floss ends to secure. Trim tassel ends.

For ornament with chamois tassel, combine and twist floss as before.

Cut enough of the cord to fit around ornament. Glue, overlapping ends on back. Fringe the 5x1-inch piece of chamois into four ¼-inch-wide fringes, leaving ½ inch uncut at top. Glue uncut edge to bottom of ornament. Slip a barrel bead over each fringe. Tie a knot below each bead.

Fold ¼-inch-wide chamois strip in half to form a loop. Tack to the top of ornament back.

Pink the edges of the chamois square. Glue the chamois square to the ornament back. Glue the flat bead to the center of the ornament.

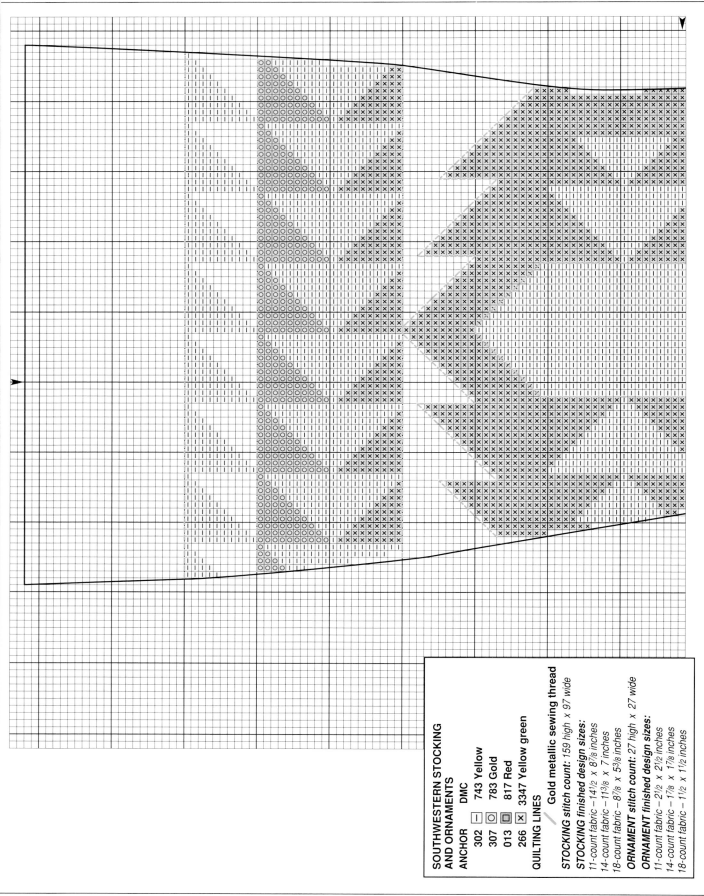

SOUTHWESTERN STOCKING
AND ORNAMENTS

ANCHOR		DMC	
302	I	743	Yellow
307	O	783	Gold
013	▨	817	Red
266	X	3347	Yellow green

QUILTING LINES

╱ Gold metallic sewing thread

STOCKING stitch count: 159 high x 97 wide

STOCKING finished design sizes:
11-count fabric – 14½ x 8⅞ inches
14-count fabric – 11⅜ x 7 inches
18-count fabric – 8⅞ x 5⅜ inches

ORNAMENT stitch count: 27 high x 27 wide

ORNAMENT finished design sizes:
11-count fabric – 2½ x 2½ inches
14-count fabric – 1⅞ x 1⅞ inches
18-count fabric – 1½ x 1½ inches

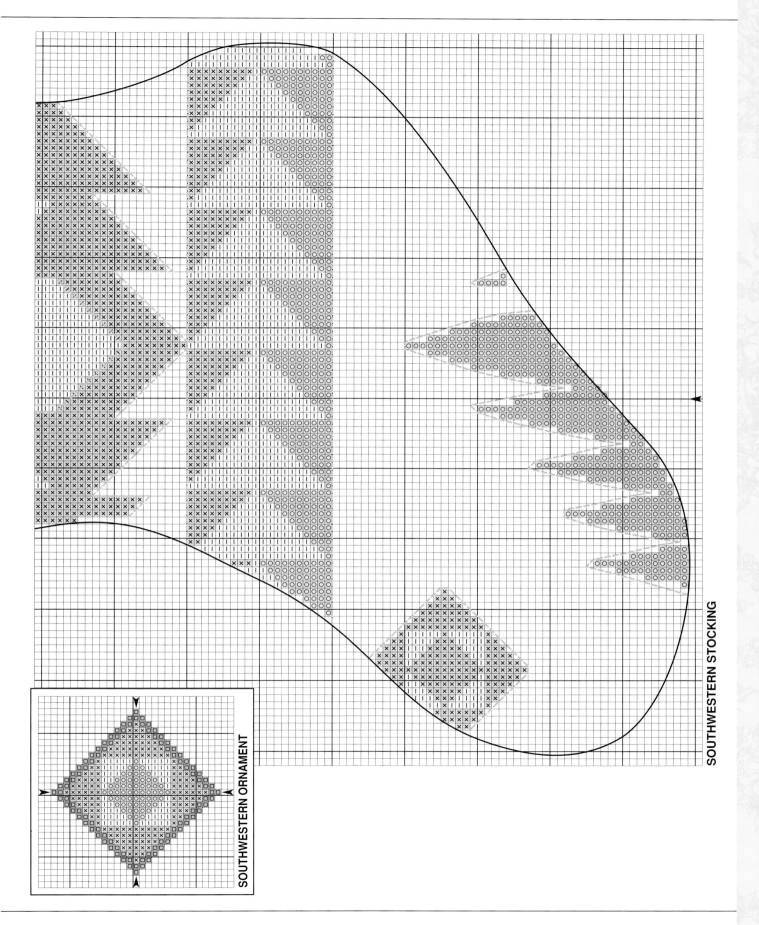

SOUTHWESTERN STOCKING

SOUTHWESTERN ORNAMENT

Stockings for Santa

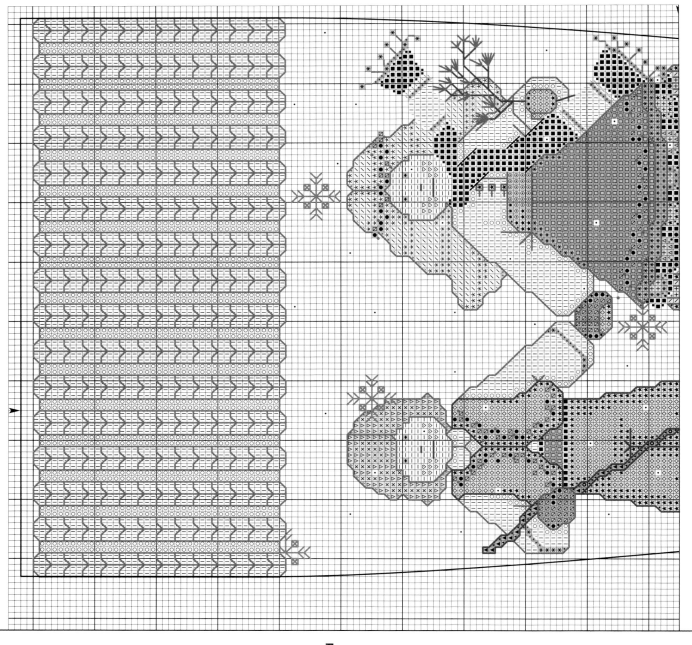

SCANDINAVIAN STOCKING

ANCHOR		DMC	
002	·	000	White
403	■	310	Black
1025	✶	347	Deep salmon
358	◀	433	Deep golden brown
310	◉	434	Medium golden brown
1045	✕	436	Dark tan
267	▨	469	Dark avocado
266	◁	471	Light avocado
1041	#	535	True ash gray
891	+	676	Light old gold
886	╱	677	Pale old gold
901	★	680	Dark old gold
926	—	712	Cream
890	◇	729	Medium old gold
361	╲	738	Light tan
885	○	739	Pale tan
380	◆	838	Deep beige brown
269	●	936	Medium pine green
1024	▢	3328	Dark salmon
1008	▷	3773	Medium rose beige

BLENDED NEEDLE

310	▷	434	Medium golden brown (1X) and
1045		436	Dark tan (1X)
1045	✶	436	Dark tan (1X) and
361		738	Light tan (1X)
901	⊙	680	Dark old gold (1X) and
891		676	Light old gold (1X)
778	—	3774	Pale rose beige (1X) and
1008		3773	Medium rose beige (1X)

BACKSTITCH

002	╱	000	White – snowflakes
403	╱	310	Black – scarf, ducks
1025	╱	347	Deep salmon – scarf, girl's dress
310	╱	434	Medium golden brown – hair, sleeves, bottom fringe on dress
361	╱	738	Light tan – borders
380	╱	838	Deep beige brown – boy's vest and pants, ducks
269	╱	936	Medium pine green – gloves

STRAIGHT STITCH

380	╱	838	Deep beige brown – branches
269	╱	936	Medium pine green – pine needles

FRENCH KNOT

1025	●	347	Deep salmon – holly on vest, dress and in girl's hair

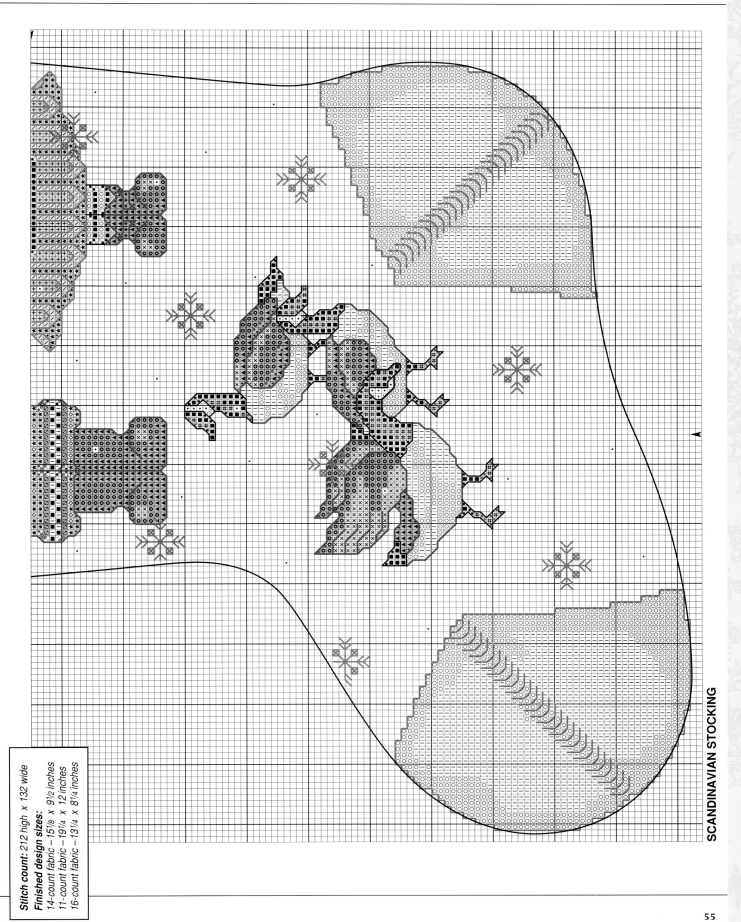

Stitch count: 212 high x 132 wide
Finished design sizes:
14-count fabric – 15⅛ x 9½ inches
11-count fabric – 19¼ x 12 inches
16-count fabric – 13¼ x 8¼ inches

SCANDINAVIAN STOCKING

★★★★ SCANDINAVIAN STOCKING

As shown on page 45, finished stocking measures 15 inches tall.

MATERIALS

FABRICS

20x15-inch piece of 28-count amaretto Jubilee fabric

¾ yard of green calico fabric

18x13-inch piece of fusible fleece

FLOSS

Cotton embroidery floss in colors listed in key on page 54

SUPPLIES

Needle; embroidery hoop

Erasable fabric marker

1½ yards of purchased metallic gold piping

7 inches of ¼-inch-wide metallic gold flat braid

1⅛ yards of ¼-inch-wide white flat lace

2⅛ yards of 1½-inch-wide green and salmon plaid ribbon

2½-inch-diameter gold filigree snowflake

INSTRUCTIONS

Tape or zigzag the edges of the Jubilee fabric to prevent fraying. Find the center of chart and the center of fabric; begin stitching there.

Use two plies of floss to work cross-stitches over two threads of fabric. Work blended needle as specified in key. Work backstitches, straight stitches, and French knots using two plies of floss.

Use marker to draw an outline as indicated on chart. Fuse fleece to back of Jubilee fabric. Cut out the stocking ¼ inch beyond line. Use Jubilee stocking as a pattern to cut one back and two lining pieces from cotton fabric.

Baste piping around sides of stocking front with raw edges even. Sew front to back, with right sides together, along the basting lines. Leave the top edge open. Turn and press.

Baste piping around top of stocking with raw edges even. Fold gold braid in half to form a loop. Tack loop to inside top right edge of stocking.

Sew lining pieces together, with right sides together, leaving top open and an opening at bottom of foot. *Do not turn.* Slip the stocking inside the lining. Stitch stocking and lining together at top edge; turn. Slip-stitch the opening closed.

Tuck lining into stocking; press carefully. Glue lace around sides of stocking behind piping.

Cut a 16-inch piece from ribbon; set aside. Make a six loop bow from remaining ribbon.

Tie center of bow with cut ribbon piece. Tack bow and snowflake to top right corner of stocking.

★★ JESTER STOCKING

As shown on page 46, finished stocking measures 13 inches tall.

MATERIALS

FABRICS

18x15-inch piece of 11-count white Aida cloth

½ yard of 45-inch-wide white cotton fabric

⅓ yard of 45-inch-wide red cotton fabric

16x12-inch piece of fleece

THREADS

Cotton embroidery floss in colors listed in key

Metallic embroidery thread in color listed in key

SUPPLIES

Needle; embroidery hoop

Erasable fabric marker; graph paper

1 yard of purchased metallic gold piping

9-inch piece of ⅛-inch-diameter metallic gold cord

Five ¾-inch-diameter jingle bells

INSTRUCTIONS

Tape or zigzag edges of fabric to prevent fraying. Find the center of chart and the center of fabric; begin stitching there.

Use four plies of floss or three strands of metallic thread to work cross-stitches. Work running stitches using two plies of floss or one strand of gold thread.

Use the marker to draw an outline as indicated on chart. Fuse the fleece to back of Aida cloth.

Cut out stocking ¼ inch beyond marker line. Use Aida cloth stocking as a pattern to cut one back from red fabric and two lining pieces from white fabric.

Enlarge the stocking cuff pattern, *below*, using the graph paper and cut out. The pattern includes ¼-inch seam allowances. Use the cuff pattern to cut two cuff pieces from the red cotton fabric.

Baste the piping around the sides and the foot of stocking front with raw edges even. Sew the front to the back with right sides together, along basting. Leave the top edge open.

Sew short ends of each cuff piece together, with right sides together and raw edges even. Sew pointed edges of cuff pieces together; clip corners. Turn right side out and press.

Baste straight edge of cuff to top of stocking with raw edges even. Fold gold cord in half to form a loop. Tack the loop to the inside top right edge of stocking.

Sew the lining pieces together, with the right sides together, leaving the top open and an opening at the bottom of foot; *do not* turn. Slip stocking inside lining.

Stitch the stocking and the lining together at the top edge; turn. Slip-stitch the opening closed. Tuck the lining into stocking. Press the stocking carefully.

Unfold cuff and topstitch around top of stocking, ⅛ inch from seam. Fold cuff over stocking. Sew jingle bells to the stocking toe and the points of the cuff.

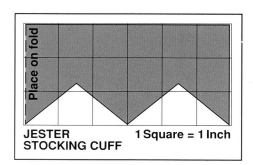

JESTER STOCKING CUFF   **1 Square = 1 Inch**

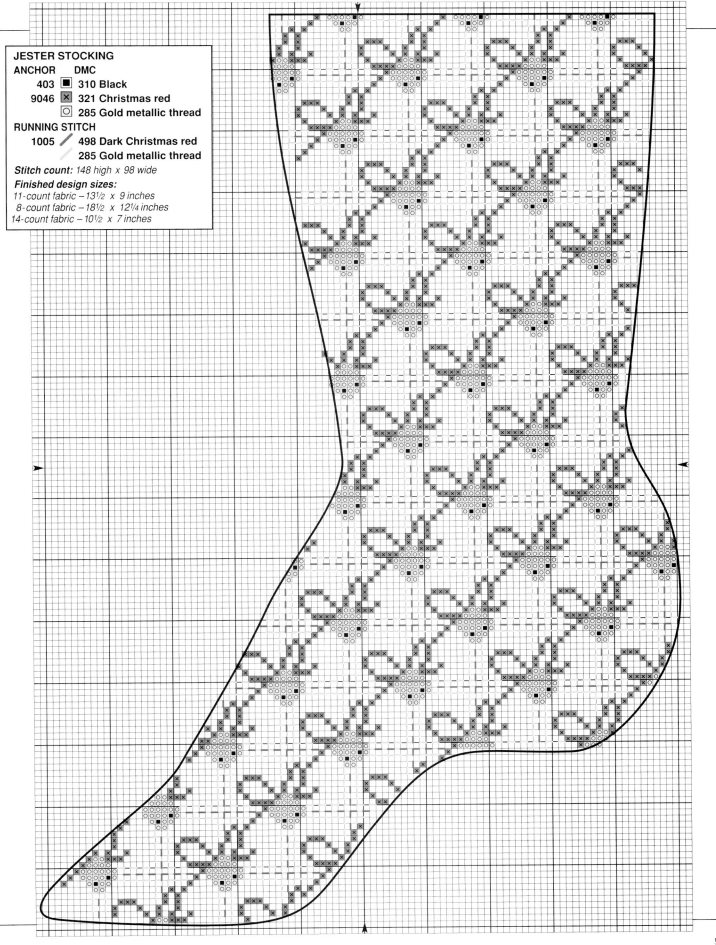

JESTER STOCKING

ANCHOR		DMC	
403	■	310	Black
9046	☒	321	Christmas red
	⊙	285	Gold metallic thread

RUNNING STITCH

| 1005 | ╱ | 498 | Dark Christmas red |
| | ╱ | 285 | Gold metallic thread |

Stitch count: 148 high x 98 wide

Finished design sizes:
11-count fabric – 13½ x 9 inches
 8-count fabric – 18½ x 12¼ inches
14-count fabric – 10½ x 7 inches

Heartwarming Gifts

*O*ne of the greatest joys of the Christmas season is the giving and receiving of specially handcrafted gifts. This lovingly stitched gift collection features festive holiday motifs as well as unique cross-stitch designs for every season of the year and every member of the family. May these merry and bright gift ideas bring the true spirit of Christmas home to you.

Merry Yule Sampler and Kitchen Accessories

Unbleached muslin creates the backdrop for these quaint country designs. Each motif is transferred onto the muslin using an iron-on transfer pen, then stitched. The jar toppers make quick decorative wrappings for delicious homemade treats—while the hot pad, bread cloth, and sampler bring holiday warmth to wherever family and friends gather. Full-size patterns and instructions begin on page 68.

DESIGNER: KATHY MOENKHAUS ● PHOTOGRAPHER: HOPKINS ASSOCIATES

Heartwarming Gifts

Fly-Fishing Case

If there's an avid fly-fisherman on your holiday gift list, this can be the best Christmas ever! This clever fly-fishing case is worked on perforated plastic for durability, then lined with shearling fabric to safely store fishing flies. Stitch the handsome design, load the case with lures, and watch for the happy smile on the face of your favorite angler. Complete instructions and chart begin on page 71.

DESIGNER: THOMPSON DESIGN STUDIO ● PHOTOGRAPHERS: RIGHT, HOPKINS ASSOCIATES; BELOW, SCOTT LITTLE

Fishing and Golf Shirts

Sports enthusiasts will love these shirts! Both the golfing and the fishing motifs are worked on two separate pieces of 14-count waste canvas—one on the pocket and one just above—for added dimension. The pocket portion is stitched through one layer of fabric so the pocket is still able to hold an extra golf tee or bobber. Complete instructions and charts for these shirts begin on page 74.

DESIGNER: JEFF JULSETH ● PHOTOGRAPHERS: RIGHT, HOPKINS ASSOCIATES; BELOW, SCOTT LITTLE

Racing Shirt and Tool Apron

Bold designs make this vivid racing shirt and handy tool apron a "must-have" in the pit or in the workshop! Stitched on waste canvas using a small palette of colors, these wearables stitch up quickly for extra-special holiday gifts—or gifts any time of the year! Complete instructions and charts for the two motifs begin on page 76.

DESIGNER: JEFF JULSETH ● PHOTOGRAPHERS: ABOVE, SCOTT LITTLE; RIGHT, HOPKINS ASSOCIATES

Elegant Jewelry Roll, Brooch, and Earrings

Flowers stitched in pastel shades of blue on white linen create this lovely gift set which is embellished with gold thread and two sizes of tiny pearls. The zippered compartments in the satin lining safely store jewelry while traveling. Finished with matching piping and satin ribbons, the jewelry roll will be a much-appreciated Christmas gift. Stitch portions of the floral motif to make a matching brooch and earrings. Complete instructions and chart begin on page 78.

DESIGNER: URSULA MICHAEL
PHOTOGRAPHER: HOPKINS ASSOCIATES

Heartwarming Gifts

Snow Family Finger Puppets

Quick to stitch on perforated plastic, this friendly snow family becomes playful finger puppets to spark the imagination of young ones all winter long. These fun designs could also be used as ornaments, or slip them over thimbles to make adorable table decorations. Complete instructions and charts for these smiling characters begin on page 80.

DESIGNER: CAROLE RODGERS ● PHOTOGRAPHER: HOPKINS ASSOCIATES

Bluebird Bear

Playtime is even more fun when there's someone to share it with! Little ones will have fun making up stories about the bird seed in this bear's hand and the bluebird on his hat. And when playtime is over, this handsome bear is just the right size for snuggling. Worked on 8-count Aida cloth, this friendly companion stitches up with ease. After the stitching is complete, sew on a fabric backing, stuff with fiberfill, and the bear is ready to be gift wrapped. Complete instructions and chart begin on page 80.

DESIGNER: SUE BANKER ● PHOTOGRAPHER: HOPKINS ASSOCIATES

MERRY YULE SAMPLER

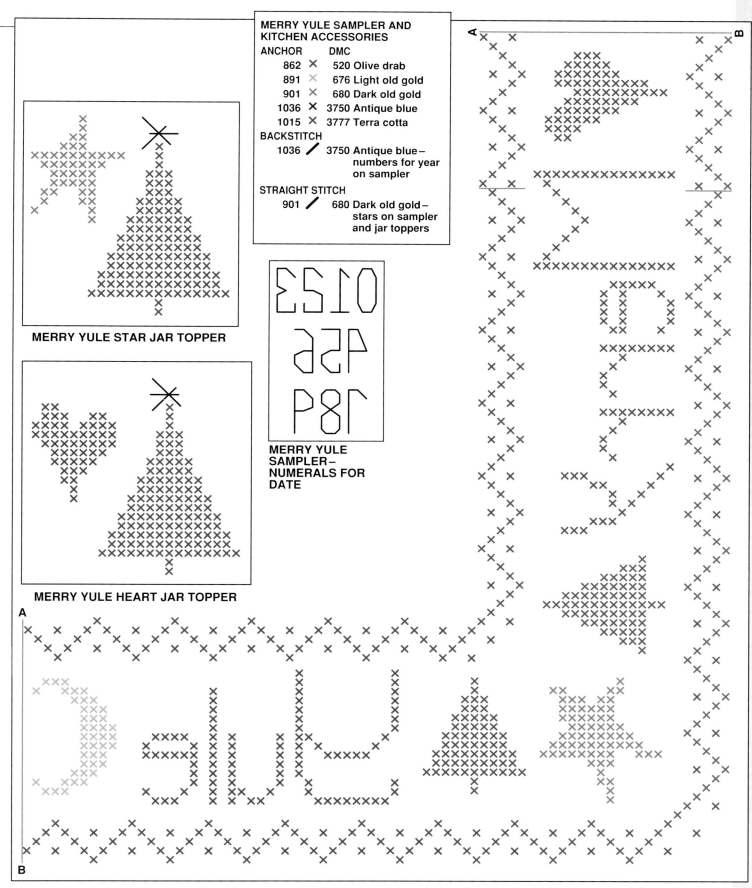

MERRY YULE SAMPLER AND KITCHEN ACCESSORIES

ANCHOR		DMC	
862	✕	520	Olive drab
891	✕	676	Light old gold
901	✕	680	Dark old gold
1036	✕	3750	Antique blue
1015	✕	3777	Terra cotta

BACKSTITCH

1036	╱	3750	Antique blue – numbers for year on sampler

STRAIGHT STITCH

901	╱	680	Dark old gold – stars on sampler and jar toppers

MERRY YULE STAR JAR TOPPER

MERRY YULE HEART JAR TOPPER

MERRY YULE SAMPLER – NUMERALS FOR DATE

MERRY YULE BREAD CLOTH

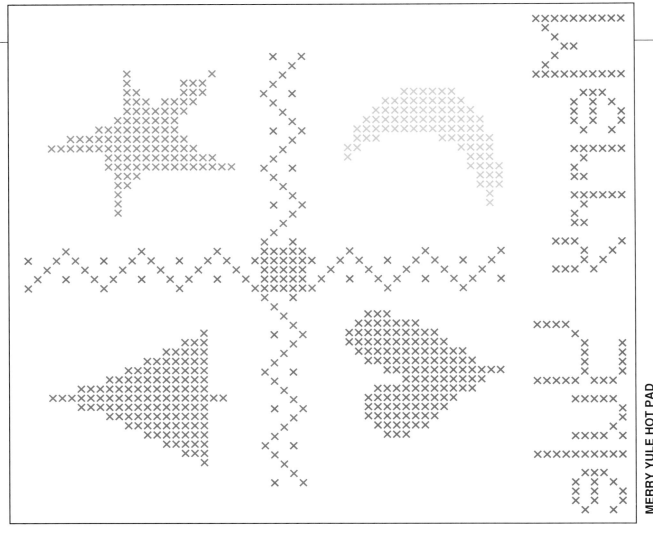

MERRY YULE HOT PAD

**MERRY YULE SAMPLER

As shown on pages 58–59.

MATERIALS
FABRIC
12x12-inch piece of unbleached muslin
FLOSS
Cotton embroidery floss in colors listed
   in key on page 69
SUPPLIES
Iron-on transfer pen; tracing paper
Needle; embroidery hoop
Mat and frame

INSTRUCTIONS
Trace pattern using iron-on pen. Center tracing on muslin, ink side down; iron as pen package directs.

Tape or zigzag edges of fabric. Use two plies of floss to work cross-stitches as marked on muslin. Work straight stitches using one ply and backstitches using two plies. Press and frame.

*BREAD CLOTH

As shown on page 58, the finished bread cloth measures 15x14½ inches.

MATERIALS
FABRIC
18x16-inch piece of unbleached
   muslin
FLOSS
Cotton embroidery floss in colors listed
   in key on page 69
SUPPLIES
Iron-on transfer pen
Tracing paper
Needle
Embroidery hoop
White sewing thread

INSTRUCTIONS
Trace the bread cloth pattern, *page 69,* using the iron-on transfer pen. To complete the bread cloth design, trace the heart motif to the left of the moon motif at the bottom left corner of the design. Do this by tracing the heart and border motifs only, omitting any portion of the letter "M." in "Merry." When tracing the heart, match points A and points B on the motif border as indicated on the bread cloth pattern on page 69.

Center the complete tracing on the unbleached muslin fabric with the ink side down. Iron as the pen package directs.

Tape or zigzag the edges of the unbleached muslin fabric to prevent fraying. Use two plies of floss to work cross-stitches as marked on the muslin. Trim the completed cross-stitched piece of muslin to measure 15x14½ inches.

For fringed edge, topstitch ¾ inch from the edge on all four sides of the stitched bread cloth. Remove the fabric threads between the cut edges and the topstitching.

**JAR TOPPERS

As shown on page 58, finished toppers fit standard canning jars.

MATERIALS *for each topper*
FABRICS
6x6-inch piece of unbleached muslin

Two 12-inch-diameter circles of red, green, and tan plaid fabric
FLOSS
Cotton embroidery floss in colors listed in key on page 69
SUPPLIES
Iron-on transfer pen; tracing paper

Needle; embroidery hoop

Erasable fabric marker

9-inch piece of ⅛-inch-wide elastic

1 yard of ⅛-inch-wide green and gold or red and gold braid trim

1⅛ yards of ⅜-inch-wide gold or burgundy rickrack

INSTRUCTIONS
Trace desired pattern, *page 69,* using iron-on transfer pen. Center tracing on muslin, ink side down; iron as transfer pen package directs.

Tape or zigzag edges of fabric. Use two plies of floss to work cross-stitches as marked on muslin. Work straight stitches using one ply.

Use erasable marker to draw a 3-inch circle on muslin, centering stitching. Stay-stitch on line. Cut out ¼ inch beyond line. Turn outside edges of circle under on stay-stitched line, clipping edges as necessary.

Baste rickrack under outside edge of muslin circle with points at one edge aligned to raw edges. Center and pin muslin on one plaid fabric circle; topstitch through all layers.

Sew rickrack to plaid circle, right sides together and points aligned to raw edge. With right sides together, sew plaid circles together leaving an opening to turn.

Clip curves, turn, and sew opening closed. Zigzag over elastic 1½ inches from outer edge of circle. Pull elastic to tighten as necessary and secure.

Place topper on jar. Wrap braid around topper; tie in large bow at front of jar. Knot ends of braid.

*HOT PAD

As shown on page 58, finished hot pad is 8½x7¾ inches.

MATERIALS
FABRICS
10x10-inch piece of unbleached muslin

Two 8½x7¾-inch pieces of heavy fleece

¼ yard of 45-inch-wide red, green, and tan plaid fabric
FLOSS
Cotton embroidery floss in colors listed in key on page 69
SUPPLIES
Iron-on transfer pen

Tracing paper

Needle

Embroidery hoop

1 yard of ⅜-inch-wide gold rickrack

INSTRUCTIONS
Trace the pattern using the iron-on pen. Center the tracing on the muslin, ink side down; iron as the pen package directs.

Tape or zigzag the edges of the muslin fabric to prevent fraying. Use two plies of floss to work cross-stitches as marked on muslin. Trim the muslin square to measure 7¾x8½ inches.

From tan plaid fabric, cut one 7¾x8½-inch back and three 2½x16-inch bias binding strips.

Layer the back, the fleece, and the stitchery. Baste the layers together. Baste rickrack around the square, with outer points ¼ inch from edges.

With right sides together, sew the short ends of the binding strips together to form one long strip. With right sides together, sew one long edge of the binding strip to edges of hot pad, using ½-inch seams and mitering corners.

Turn remaining raw edge of binding under ½ inch. Fold the fabric to back. Mitering corners, slip stitch fabric to back of the hot pad.

Fold the remaining rickrack in half to make a loop; tack to the top corner of the hot pad.

***FLY-FISHING CASE

As shown on pages 60–61, finished fly-fishing case is 8½x11 inches.

MATERIALS
FABRICS
9x12-inch piece of 14-count clear perforated plastic

8½x11-inch piece of shearling fabric
THREADS
Cotton embroidery floss in colors listed in key on page 73

3 additional skeins of drab brown (DMC 613)

1 additional skein of black (DMC 310)

Blending filament as listed in key on page 73
SUPPLIES
Needle

Two 1x1-inch squares of tan Velcro

Tan sewing thread

INSTRUCTIONS
Find center of the chart and center of the perforated plastic; begin stitching there. Work all cross-stitches before working the half cross-stitches of the background.

Use three plies of floss to work cross-stitches. Work half cross-stitches in the direction of symbol using six plies of floss. Work the backstitches using one ply of floss unless otherwise specified in the key.

Trim the excess perforated plastic one square beyond the stitching. Use six plies of black floss to work overcast stitches around the edges of the fishing case design.

Pin the shearling fabric to the stitched piece with the wrong sides together. Turn the edges of the shearling under ¼ inch and use a doubled length of tan sewing thread to whipstitch the shearling to the back of the stitched design.

With fish motif right side up, hand-sew each of the two hooked squares of Velcro to the stitched fishing case design, ¼ inch from bottom edge and 1¼ inches from each side. Sew the two looped pieces of Velcro to shearling side of fishing case, opposite the hooked squares.

Stitch count: *151 high x 113 wide*
Finished design sizes:
14-count fabric – 10³/₄ x 8¹/₈ inches
10-count fabric – 15¹/₈ x 11³/₈ inches

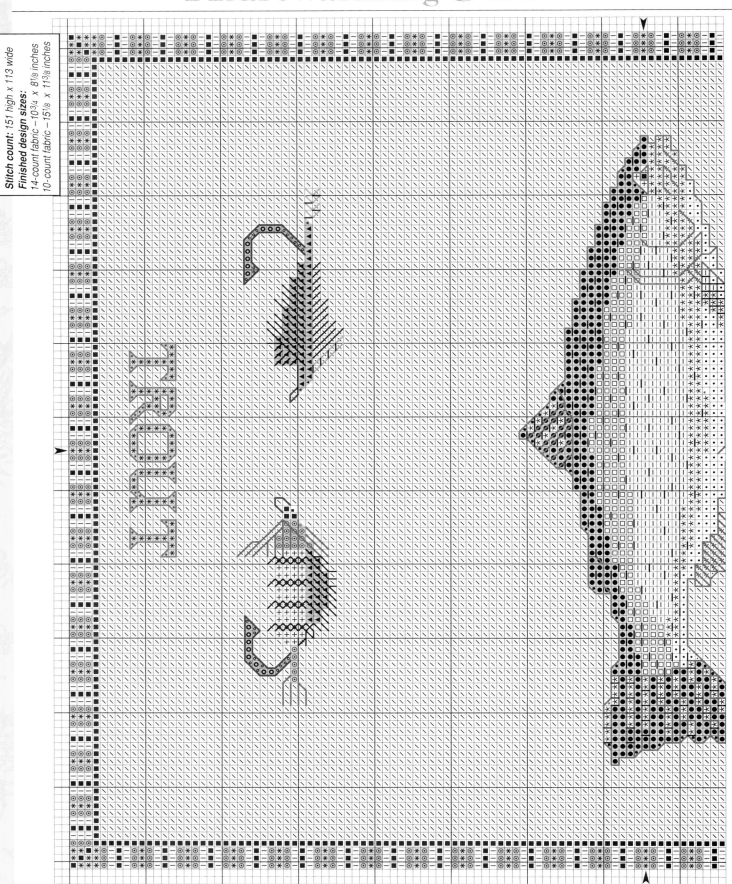

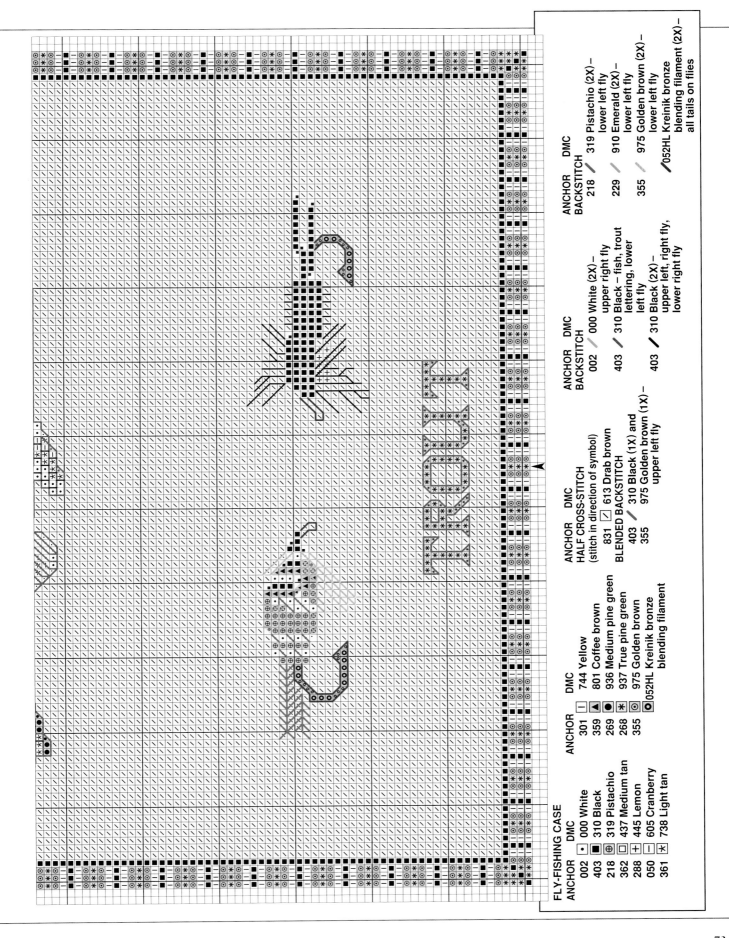

FLY-FISHING CASE

ANCHOR	DMC		ANCHOR	DMC	
002	•	000 White	301		744 Yellow
403	■	310 Black	359	◀	801 Coffee brown
218	⊕	319 Pistachio	269	●	936 Medium pine green
362	☐	437 Medium tan	268	✳	937 True pine green
288	+	445 Lemon	355	⊙	975 Golden brown
050	⊟	605 Cranberry		◉	052HL Kreinik bronze
361	✳	738 Light tan			blending filament

ANCHOR DMC
HALF CROSS-STITCH
(stitch in direction of symbol)
831 ☑ 613 Drab brown
BLENDED BACKSTITCH
403 / 310 Black (1X) and
355 975 Golden brown (1X) –
upper left fly

ANCHOR DMC
BACKSTITCH
002 / 000 White (2X) –
upper right fly
403 / 310 Black – fish, trout
lettering, lower
left fly
403 / 310 Black (2X) –
upper left, right fly,
lower right fly

ANCHOR DMC
BACKSTITCH
218 / 319 Pistachio (2X) –
lower left fly
229 / 910 Emerald (2X) –
lower left fly
355 / 975 Golden brown (2X) –
lower left fly
/ 052HL Kreinik bronze
blending filament (2X) –
all tails on flies

73

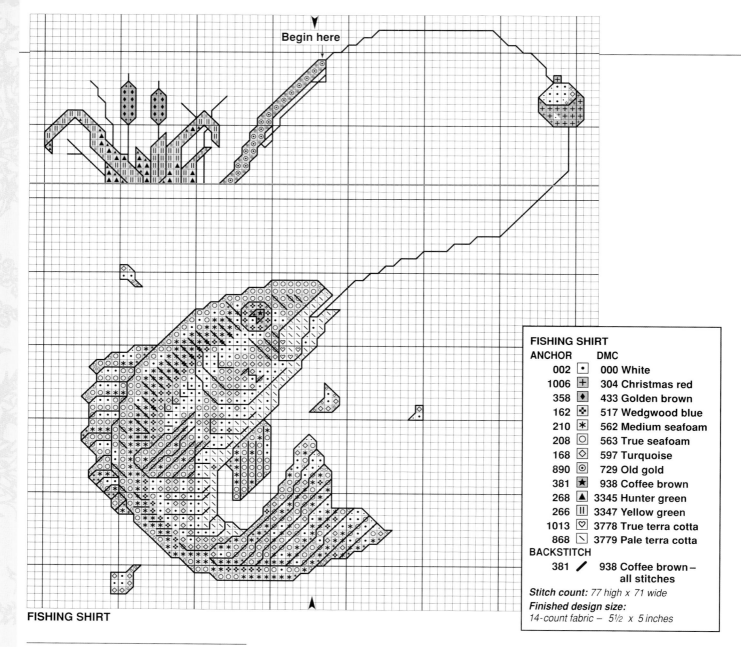

Begin here

FISHING SHIRT

FISHING SHIRT		
ANCHOR		**DMC**
002	⬚	000 White
1006	✚	304 Christmas red
358	◆	433 Golden brown
162	❖	517 Wedgwood blue
210	✳	562 Medium seafoam
208	○	563 True seafoam
168	◇	597 Turquoise
890	◉	729 Old gold
381	★	938 Coffee brown
268	▲	3345 Hunter green
266	‖	3347 Yellow green
1013	♡	3778 True terra cotta
868	◵	3779 Pale terra cotta
BACKSTITCH		
381	╱	938 Coffee brown – all stitches

Stitch count: 77 high x 71 wide
Finished design size:
14-count fabric – 5½ x 5 inches

✱✱FISHING SHIRT

As shown on page 62, pocket motif is 5¹⁄₂x5 inches.

MATERIALS
FABRICS
Purchased chambray shirt with 5½-inch-wide or larger pocket
Two 7x7-inch pieces of 14-count waste canvas
3½x5½-inch piece of lightweight fusible interfacing
FLOSS
Cotton embroidery floss in colors listed in key
SUPPLIES
Needle; basting thread; tweezers

INSTRUCTIONS

Wash and dry shirt. Zigzag edges of waste canvas to prevent fraying.

Baste one piece of waste canvas to shirt above pocket, centering left to right with four squares of waste canvas tucked into shirt pocket. Make a vertical clip four squares deep in waste canvas where it meets pocket seams, if needed.

Find the beginning stitch on the chart and the vertical center of the waste canvas; begin stitching 1¼ inches above edge of pocket.

Use three plies of floss to work cross-stitches. Work backstitches using one ply. Remove basting threads; trim canvas close to stitching.

Wet waste canvas. Using tweezers, pull the individual threads from under the stitches.

Baste remaining piece of waste canvas to pocket, centering left to right with top edge of canvas ¼ inch above top edge of pocket. *Do not stitch through shirt fabric if use of pocket is desired.* Locate point where fishing line motif meets; begin stitching on pocket there.

Remove the basting threads; trim canvas close to stitching. Wet the canvas and remove the individual threads in the same manner as for shirt.

Fuse the interfacing over stitching on the inside of the shirt following the manufacturer's instructions.

★★GOLF SHIRT

As shown on page 62, pocket motif is 7⅝x4 inches.

MATERIALS

FABRICS
Purchased green knit shirt with pocket
One 6x6-inch piece and one 4x3-inch
piece of 14-count waste canvas
5x5-inch piece of lightweight fusible
interfacing

FLOSS
Cotton embroidery floss in colors listed
in key

SUPPLIES
Needle; basting thread; tweezers

INSTRUCTIONS

Wash and dry shirt. Zigzag edges of waste canvas to prevent fraying.

Baste larger piece of waste canvas to shirt above pocket, centering left to right with four squares of waste canvas tucked into shirt pocket. Make a vertical clip four squares deep in waste canvas where it meets pocket seams, if needed.

Find center of golf club motif and vertical center of waste canvas; begin stitching 2 inches above edge of pocket.

Use three plies of floss to work cross-stitches. Work backstitches using one ply of floss. Remove basting threads; trim canvas close to stitching. Wet the canvas; using tweezers, pull individual threads from under the cross-stitches.

Center and baste remaining piece of waste canvas to pocket. *Do not* stitch through shirt fabric if use of pocket is desired. Find top left stitch on golf ball and vertical center of canvas; begin stitching 2 inches down from pocket edge.

Remove basting threads; trim canvas close to stitching. Wet the canvas, and remove threads as for shirt.

Fuse interfacing over stitching on inside of shirt following manufacturer's instructions.

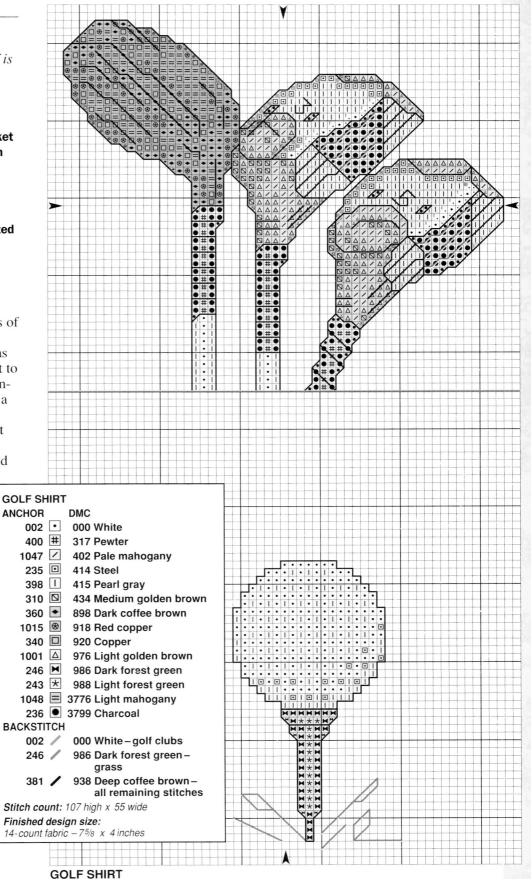

GOLF SHIRT

GOLF SHIRT		
ANCHOR		DMC
002	·	000 White
400	#	317 Pewter
1047	╱	402 Pale mahogany
235	▣	414 Steel
398	∣	415 Pearl gray
310	◩	434 Medium golden brown
360	◆	898 Dark coffee brown
1015	⊛	918 Red copper
340	▢	920 Copper
1001	△	976 Light golden brown
246	⋈	986 Dark forest green
243	✶	988 Light forest green
1048	▤	3776 Light mahogany
236	●	3799 Charcoal
BACKSTITCH		
002	╱	000 White — golf clubs
246	╱	986 Dark forest green — grass
381	╱	938 Deep coffee brown — all remaining stitches

Stitch count: 107 high x 55 wide
Finished design size:
14-count fabric – 7⅝ x 4 inches

GOLF SHIRT

★★RACING SHIRT

As shown on page 63, pocket motif is 5³⁄₄x4¹⁄₈ inches.

MATERIALS

FABRICS
Purchased red knit shirt with 4½-inch-wide or larger pocket
Two 6x6-inch pieces of 14-count waste canvas
3½x5-inch piece of lightweight fusible interfacing

FLOSS
Cotton embroidery floss in colors listed in key

SUPPLIES
Needle
Basting thread
Tweezers

INSTRUCTIONS

Wash and dry the shirt. Zigzag the edges of the waste canvas to prevent it from fraying.

Baste one piece of the waste canvas to the shirt above the pocket, centering left to right with four squares of the waste canvas tucked into the shirt pocket. Make a vertical clip four squares deep in the waste canvas where it meets pocket seams, if needed.

Find the beginning cross-stitch on the chart and the vertical center of the waste canvas; begin stitching 1⅛ inches above the edge of the shirt pocket.

Use three plies of floss to work cross-stitches. Work backstitches using one ply of floss.

Remove the basting threads and trim the waste canvas close to the stitching. Wet waste canvas. Using tweezers, pull individual waste canvas threads from under cross-stitches.

Baste the remaining piece of waste canvas to the shirt pocket, centering left to right with the top edge of the waste canvas ¼ inch above the top edge of the shirt pocket. *Do not* stitch through shirt fabric if use of pocket is desired.

Locate the point where the hand and the racing flag handle motifs

meet; begin stitching on the shirt pocket there.

Remove the basting threads; trim the waste canvas close to the stitching. Wet the waste canvas and using tweezers, pull individual threads from under the cross-stitches.

Fuse the interfacing over the stitching on the inside of the shirt following the manufacturer's instructions.

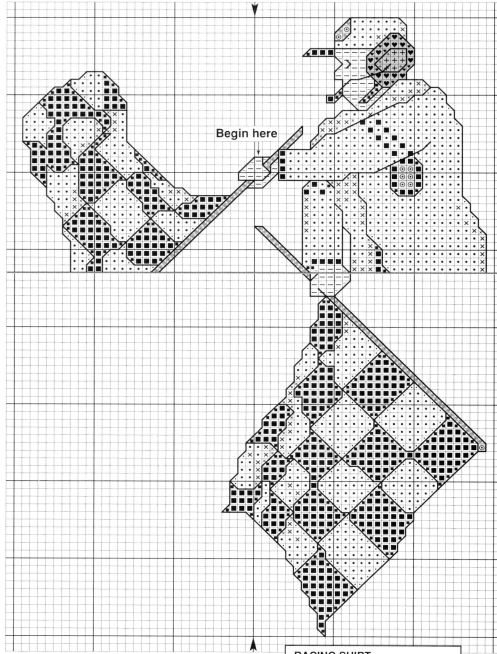

Begin here

RACING SHIRT

RACING SHIRT		
ANCHOR		**DMC**
002	·	000 White
1006	+	304 Christmas red
403	■	310 Black
399	✕	318 Steel
890	⊙	729 Old gold
045	♥	814 Garnet
881	–	945 Ivory
BACKSTITCH		
381	╱	938 Coffee brown – all stitches

Stitch count: 80 high x 58 wide
Finished design size:
14-count fabric – 5³⁄₄ x 4¹⁄₈ inches

★★TOOL APRON

As shown on page 63, pocket motif is 8¼x4 inches.

MATERIALS

FABRICS
Purchased ivory duck apron with a 4¾-inch-wide or larger pocket
One 6x5-inch and one 3½x3-inch piece of 14-count waste canvas
5x4-inch piece of lightweight fusible interfacing

FLOSS
Cotton embroidery floss in colors listed in key

SUPPLIES
Needle; basting thread; tweezers

INSTRUCTIONS

Wash and dry apron. Zigzag edges of waste canvas to prevent fraying.

Baste larger piece of waste canvas to apron above pocket, centering left to right with four squares of waste canvas tucked into apron pocket. Make a vertical clip four squares deep in waste canvas where it meets pocket seams, if needed.

Find center of tool motif and vertical center of waste canvas; begin stitching 2 inches above edge of apron pocket.

Use three plies of floss to work cross-stitches. Work backstitches using one ply of floss. Remove basting threads; trim canvas close to stitching. Wet the canvas; using tweezers, pull individual threads from under the cross-stitches.

Center and baste the remaining piece of waste canvas to right half of pocket. *Do not* stitch through apron fabric if use of pocket is desired. Begin stitching top left stitch on vertical screw 1¾ inches down from the top of pocket and 2½ inches from the left edge.

Remove basting threads; trim canvas close to stitching. Wet the canvas, and remove threads in the same manner as for apron.

Fuse interfacing over stitching on inside of apron following the manufacturer's instructions.

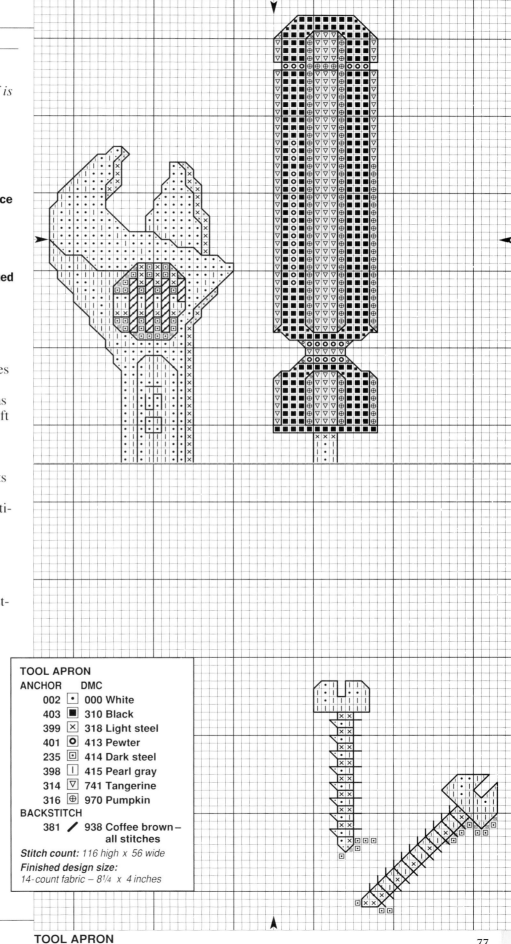

TOOL APRON		
ANCHOR		**DMC**
002	·	000 White
403	■	310 Black
399	☒	318 Light steel
401	◉	413 Pewter
235	▣	414 Dark steel
398	Ι	415 Pearl gray
314	▽	741 Tangerine
316	⊕	970 Pumpkin
BACKSTITCH		
381	╱	938 Coffee brown – all stitches

Stitch count: 116 high x 56 wide
Finished design size:
14-count fabric – 8¼ x 4 inches

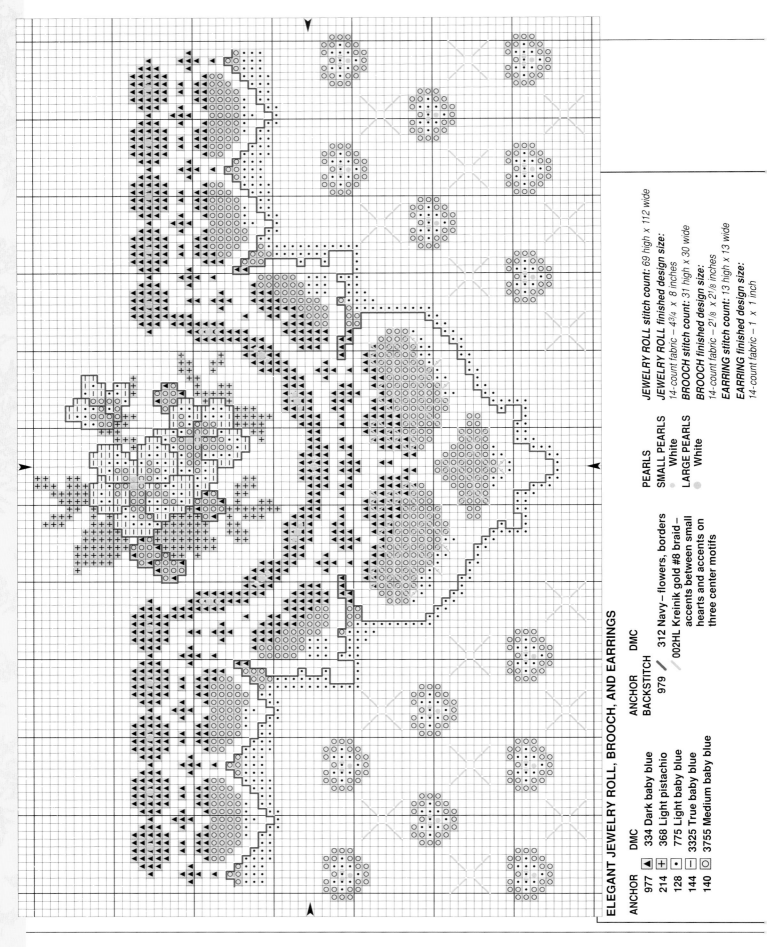

ELEGANT JEWELRY ROLL, BROOCH, AND EARRINGS

ANCHOR	DMC	
977	◀	Dark baby blue
214	+	Light pistachio
128	•	Light baby blue
144	—	True baby blue
140	◎	Medium baby blue

ANCHOR	DMC	
BACKSTITCH		
979	╱	312 Navy—flowers, borders
	╱	002HL Kreinik gold #8 braid— accents between small hearts and accents on three center motifs

PEARLS

SMALL PEARLS
  • White

LARGE PEARLS
  ● White

JEWELRY ROLL stitch count: 69 high x 112 wide

JEWELRY ROLL finished design size:
14-count fabric — 4³/₄ x 8 inches

BROOCH stitch count: 31 high x 30 wide

BROOCH finished design size:
14-count fabric — 2¹/₈ x 2¹/₈ inches

EARRING stitch count: 13 high x 13 wide

EARRING finished design size:
14-count fabric — 1 x 1 inch

★★ JEWELRY ROLL

As shown on pages 64–65, finished jewelry roll is 14½x8⅞ inches.

MATERIALS
FABRICS
18x12-inch piece of 28-count white linen
½ yard of 45-inch-wide light blue satin
15¼x9¾-inch piece of fleece
THREADS
Cotton embroidery floss and metallic braid in colors listed in key
SUPPLIES
Needle; embroidery hoop
White and light blue sewing thread
Eighty-two 2.5-millimeter pearls
Seventeen 4-millimeter pearls
1½ yards of ⅛-inch-diameter cording
Two 9-inch-long zippers
2 yards of ⅛-inch-wide light blue satin ribbon

INSTRUCTIONS
Tape or zigzag edges of linen. Find vertical center of chart and of fabric; begin stitching top of motif 7 inches from bottom edge of fabric.

Use three plies of floss to work cross-stitches over two threads of fabric. Work backstitches using one ply of floss or two strands of braid. Use white thread to attach pearls.

Trim ⅝ inch below the bottom row of gold backstitches. Trim remaining sides so the piece measures 14¾x9½ inches. Round corners evenly. Pin fleece to wrong side of linen and machine baste ⅛ inch from edge of linen. Trim fleece even with linen.

Use linen as a pattern to cut one satin lining. Also from the linen, cut a 7¾x9½-inch top pocket, a 4¾x9½-inch middle pocket, a 3¾x9½-inch bottom pocket, and two 1¼x25-inch bias piping strips. All measurements include ⅜-inch seam allowances.

Sew two short ends of piping strips together. Center cording lengthwise on wrong side of piping strip. Fold fabric around cording bringing raw edges together. Use zipper foot to sew through both layers of fabric close to cording. Beginning at one end of fabric, with raw edges even, pin covered piping to outer edges of linen. Use a zipper foot to machine-baste.

Press one 9½-inch edge of top and bottom pockets under ⅜ inch. Press both 9½-inch edges of middle pocket under ⅜ inch. Center pressed edge of top pocket close to teeth of one zipper; baste. Baste one pressed edge of middle pocket close to teeth on other size of zipper. Baste remaining zipper between other pressed edge of middle pocket and pressed edge of bottom pocket. Use a zipper foot to sew close to pressed edges.

Pin wrong side of pocket-zipper piece to right side of satin lining, raw edges even. Baste through all layers ⅜ inch from raw edges. Trim corners of pocket-zipper piece to match lining. Machine-stitch again, through all layers, along pressed edge at bottom of middle pocket. If desired, add vertical stitching to make smaller pockets.

Cut ribbon into two equal pieces. Fold each ribbon 12 inches from one end. Pin the fold even with raw edges at center of top edge of top pocket.

Sew linen and satin pieces together with right sides facing, leaving an opening to turn. Clip curves and turn. Press; sew opening closed. Knot ribbon ends and trim diagonally.

★ BROOCH

As shown on page 64, brooch is 2½ inches in diameter.

MATERIALS
FABRICS
6x6-inch piece of 28-count white linen
4x4-inch piece of lightweight fusible interfacing
THREADS
Cotton embroidery floss in colors listed in key
#8 braid in color listed in key
SUPPLIES
Six 2.5-millimeter pearls
2½-inch-diameter button form
¼ yard of ⅛-inch-diameter blue rattail cord
¼ yard of ½-inch-wide white flat lace
Crafts glue; pin back; wire cutters
Fine sandpaper; all-purpose cement

INSTRUCTIONS
Tape or zigzag edges of fabric to prevent fraying. Find center of flower motif and center of fabric; begin stitching there.

Use three plies of floss to work cross-stitches over two threads of linen fabric. Work backstitches using one ply of floss. Use one ply of white floss to sew three pearls to each of flower centers.

Press linen on wrong side. Center interfacing on back of stitched piece and fuse following manufacturer's instructions.

Centering motif over button form, trim fabric ½ inch beyond edge. Run a gathering thread ¼ inch from cut edge. Pull thread to smooth linen around top of form.

Assemble button back following manufacturer's instructions. Glue ends of cord to prevent fraying. Beginning at top of brooch, glue cord around outer edge of brooch overlapping ends at bottom and glue raw edges to back.

Glue lace to back of brooch behind cord. Use wire cutters to remove button shank. Sand center back of button form. Using cement, glue pin back to button form.

★ EARRINGS

As shown on page 64, earrings are 1⅛ inches in diameter.

MATERIALS
FABRICS
6x8-inch piece of 28-count white linen
3x6-inch piece of lightweight fusible interfacing
THREADS
Cotton embroidery floss in colors listed in key
Metallic braid in color listed in key
SUPPLIES
Six 2-millimeter pearls; crafts glue
⅜ yard of ¹⁄₁₆-inch-diameter blue rattail cord
Two 1⅛-inch-diameter button forms
Earring backs; wire cutters
Fine sandpaper; all purpose-cement

INSTRUCTIONS

Tape or zigzag edges of fabric to prevent fraying. Centering small floral motif on one half of linen, work cross-stitches using three plies of floss over two threads of fabric. Work backstitches using one ply of floss. Use two plies of light baby blue floss to sew pearls to flower centers.

Press linen on wrong side. Center interfacing on back of stitched piece and fuse following manufacturer's instructions. Center one motif over one button form, trim fabric ½ inch beyond edge. Run a gathering thread ¼ inch from cut edge. Pull thread to smooth linen around top of form. Repeat with remaining motif and button form.

Assemble button backs following manufacturer's instructions. Cut cord into two equal pieces; glue ends to prevent fraying. Beginning at top of earring, glue cord around edge of each earring. Use wire cutters to remove button shanks. Sand center back of button forms. Using cement, glue earring backs to button forms.

★SNOW FAMILY FINGER PUPPETS

As shown on page 66, finger puppets are 3⅜ to 4⅛ inches tall.

MATERIALS *for each puppet*
FABRIC
Two 5x4-inch pieces of 14-count clear perforated plastic
THREADS
Cotton embroidery floss in colors listed in key
Metallic cable in color listed in key
SUPPLIES
Needle

INSTRUCTIONS

Find the center of the chart and the center of the perforated plastic; begin stitching there. Use two plies of floss or one strand of cable to work cross-stitches. Work backstitches using one ply of floss.

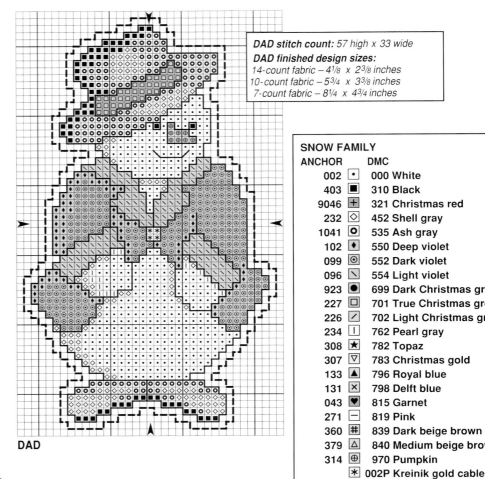

DAD

Trim plastic one square beyond the stitched area as shown on chart. Use stitched piece as a pattern to cut a back from remaining plastic. Whip-stitch pieces together using six plies of black floss, leaving bottom open.

★★BLUEBIRD BEAR

As shown on page 67, finished bear is 11 inches tall.

MATERIALS
FABRICS
16x9-inch piece of 8-count Aida cloth
13x7-inch piece of cotton fabric
THREADS
Cotton embroidery floss in colors listed in key
#8 metallic braid in color listed in key
SUPPLIES
Needle; embroidery hoop
Sewing thread
Polyester fiberfill

DAD stitch count: 57 high x 33 wide
DAD finished design sizes:
14-count fabric – 4⅛ x 2⅜ inches
10-count fabric – 5¾ x 3⅜ inches
7-count fabric – 8¼ x 4¾ inches

SNOW FAMILY

ANCHOR		DMC	
002	·	000	White
403	■	310	Black
9046	+	321	Christmas red
232	◇	452	Shell gray
1041	O	535	Ash gray
102	◆	550	Deep violet
099	◉	552	Dark violet
096	◥	554	Light violet
923	●	699	Dark Christmas green
227	□	701	True Christmas green
226	╱	702	Light Christmas green
234	‖	762	Pearl gray
308	★	782	Topaz
307	▽	783	Christmas gold
133	▲	796	Royal blue
131	✕	798	Delft blue
043	♥	815	Garnet
271	—	819	Pink
360	⊞	839	Dark beige brown
379	△	840	Medium beige brown
314	⊕	970	Pumpkin
	✳	002P	Kreinik gold cable
BACKSTITCH			
403	╱	310	Black – all stitches

INSTRUCTIONS

Tape or zigzag the edges of the Aida fabric to prevent fraying. Find the center of the chart and the center of the fabric; begin stitching there.

Use four plies of floss to work cross-stitches. Work backstitches using two plies of floss or one strand of braid. Press finished stitchery from the back.

Trim Aida cloth ½ inch beyond stitched area of design. Use Aida cloth as a pattern to cut a back from cotton fabric. Sew bear front to back with right sides together using ½-inch seams, leaving an opening to turn.

Clip the corners and curves; turn right side out. Stuff bear firmly with polyester fiberfill and sew the opening closed.

CHILD

| CHILD stitch count: 46 high x 27 wide |
| CHILD finished design sizes: |
| 14-count fabric – 3⅜ x 2 inches |
| 10-count fabric – 4⅜ x 2¾ inches |
| 7-count fabric – 6⅝ x 3⅞ inches |

| MOM stitch count: 52 high x 33 wide |
| MOM finished design sizes: |
| 14-count fabric – 3¾ x 2⅜ inches |
| 10-count fabric – 5¼ x 3⅜ inches |
| 7-count fabric – 7½ x 4¾ inches |

MOM

BLUEBIRD BEAR

ANCHOR	DMC	
002	000	White
403	310	Black
117	341	Periwinkle
008	353	Dark peach
088	718	Light plum
314	741	Tangerine
302	743	Yellow
1029	915	Dark plum
089	917	Medium plum
188	943	Dark aqua
1011	948	Light peach
187	958	True aqua
185	964	Light aqua
410	995	Dark electric blue
433	996	Medium electric blue
087	3607	Dark fuchsia
086	3608	Medium fuchsia
085	3609	Light fuchsia
1007	3772	Dark cocoa

ANCHOR	DMC	
1008	3773	Medium rose beige
778	3774	Pale rose beige

BACKSTITCH

ANCHOR	DMC	
410	995	Dark electric blue – bird's tail feathers
	202HL	Kreinik aztec gold #8 fine braid – pocket watch and chain
403	310	Black – all remaining stitches

FRENCH KNOT

ANCHOR	DMC	
403	310	Black – small bear's eyes, nose, mouth and bird's eye
936	632	Deep cocoa – large bear's nose

Stitch count: 89 high x 43 wide
Finished design sizes:
8-count fabric – 11⅛ x 5⅜ inches
11-count fabric – 8 x 3⅞ inches
14-count fabric – 6⅜ x 3 inches

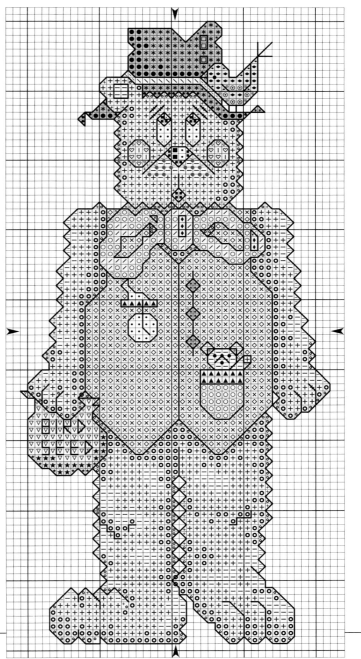

BLUEBIRD BEAR

Festive Fashion

This holiday season, dress in spectacular style with our out-of-the-ordinary array of cross-stitched wearables. For casual days of shopping and gift wrapping, create striking snowflakes on a black vest. For your next formal Christmas party, catch everyone's eye with a glorious holly and berry cummerbund with matching earrings and button covers. Come discover sensational fashion designs for everyone in your family, perfect gifts you can stitch with love.

Snowflake Vest and Snowman, Santa, and Angel Pins

Sparkling snowflakes swirl in brilliant patterns on this purchased black Lugana vest. Stitched randomly, you can repeat as many of the five snowflake designs as you'd like using opal braided ribbon. To add whimsy to your shirt collar or coat lapel, stitch up any of our trio of sweet little pins on perforated paper. Accent them with metallic thread, beads, and sequins for that extra-special holiday touch. Instructions and charts begin on page 90.

DESIGNERS: VEST, BARBARA SESTOK; PINS, SHARON BARRETT
PHOTOGRAPHER: HOPKINS ASSOCIATES

Tasseled Treasures

White perforated paper is transformed into dazzling holiday jewelry when these quick-stitch designs are worked in red, green, and gold metallic threads. For silver lovers, replace the gold stitches with silver metallic thread. Or stitch both colors and glue back to back for unique reversible accessories. Tassels made from the same threads add extra shimmer to the set. Instructions and charts begin on page 92.

DESIGNER: KAREN TAYLOR
PHOTOGRAPHER: HOPKINS ASSOCIATES

Christmas Party Cummerbund, Button Covers, and Earrings

You'll be a sparkling hostess (or guest!) when wearing these elegant wardrobe accessories. Our striking holly and berry designs are exquisite when Worked on 25-count black Lugana fabric and accented in metallic thread. Gold torsade trim and tiny gold pailletes add rich polish to these sophisticated yuletide designs. Complete instructions and charts for the cummerbund, button covers, and earrings begin on page 93.

DESIGNER: RUTH SCHMUFF ● PHOTOGRAPHER: SCOTT LITTLE

Reindeer Sweater

Prancing deer and crisp white snowflake medallions turn a solid blue
sweater into a great-looking addition to any wardrobe. A versatile motif for either
men or women, this duplicate-stitch design simply uses six plies of ecru and rose
beige floss. The soft hues of this design will get attention all winter long on a variety
of sweater colors. Complete instructions and chart are on page 95.

DESIGNER: JEFF JULSETH ● PHOTOGRAPHER: HOPKINS ASSOCIATES

Sweetheart Holiday Collar

Children love the excitement of getting dressed up, especially at Christmastime. This holiday season, make your little angel feel extra special by stitching this charming holiday collar. The design is cross-stitched on a purchased linen collar so the only finishing is to sew on the three matching heart buttons. A plain chambray dress provides the perfect backdrop for this sweetheart of a design. Instructions and chart begin on page 95.

DESIGNER: URSULA MICHAEL
PHOTOGRAPHER: HOPKINS ASSOCIATES

Festive Fashion

Friendship Mittens

There's no better way to protect cold hands than a chill-chasing pair of mittens. This heart and floral motif is worked in just a few colors, so you can easily customize the design using each friend's favorite colors. And because our fancy mittens are stitched with braided ribbon, there's no need to separate floss plies. This delightful design works up so quickly, you'll want to stitch a pair for each of your friends! Instructions and chart are on page 96.

DESIGNER: ALICE OKON ● PHOTOGRAPHER: SCOTT LITTLE

The adorable snowman pattern is easy to stitch using waste canvas and will be done in plenty of time to beat the arrival of the first snowflakes! Our frolicking fellow would also be adorable on a tree skirt, hot pads, or table runner. Instructions and chart are on page 97.

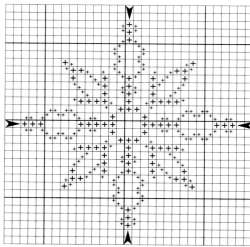

SNOWFLAKE 1

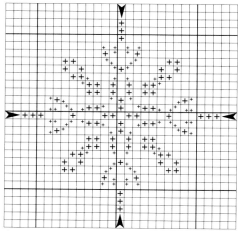

SNOWFLAKE 4

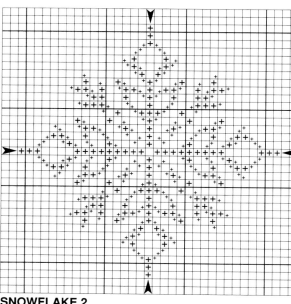

SNOWFLAKE 2

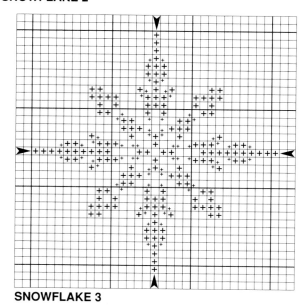

SNOWFLAKE 3

SNOWFLAKE VEST

RIBBONFLOSS

+ 144F-10 Opal Ribbonfloss or 3200 Kreinik solid pearl ombre metallic thread

SNOWFLAKE 1 stitch count:
27 high x 27 wide

SNOWFLAKE 1 finished design size:
12¹/₂-count fabric – 2¹/₈ x 2¹/₈ inches

SNOWFLAKE 2 stitch count:
33 high x 33 wide

SNOWFLAKE 2 finished design size:
12¹/₂-count fabric – 2⁵/₈ x 2⁵/₈ inches

SNOWFLAKE 3 stitch count:
31 high x 31 wide

SNOWFLAKE 3 finished design size:
12¹/₂-count fabric – 2¹/₂ x 2¹/₂ inches

SNOWFLAKE 4 stitch count:
21 high x 21 wide

SNOWFLAKE 4 finished design size:
12¹/₂-count fabric – 1⁵/₈ x 1⁵/₈ inches

SNOWFLAKE 5 stitch count:
25 high x 25 wide

SNOWFLAKE 5 finished design size:
12¹/₂-count fabric – 2 x 2 inches

SNOWFLAKE 5

★★★SNOWFLAKE VEST

As shown on page 82, 5 spools of Ribbonfloss were used.

MATERIALS

FABRIC
Purchased 25-count black Lugana vest or purchased vest pattern and 25-count fabric

THREAD
Ribbonfloss braided ribbon in color listed in key or pearl (Kreinik 032) 1/16-inch ribbon

SUPPLIES
Needle

INSTRUCTIONS

Measure 6½ inches from bottom point and 1½ inches from side seam of one side of vest; begin stitching bottom stitch of one snowflake motif there. Use one strand of braided ribbon or 1/16-inch ribbon to work cross-stitches over two threads of the fabric.

Work snowflake motifs in a random pattern on each side of vest, spacing motifs ½ to ¾ inches apart, stitching as many snowflakes as desired. Press finished vest from the back.

★★SANTA PIN

As shown on page 83, finished Santa is 2¼ inches tall.

MATERIALS

FABRICS
4x4-inch piece of 14-count gold perforated paper
2½x2½-inch piece of white felt

THREADS
Cotton embroidery floss in colors listed in key on page 92
Blending thread in colors listed in key on page 92
Metallic embroidery thread in color listed in key on page 92

SUPPLIES
Needle; crafts glue
Scissors
Red rocaille bead; silver heart sequin
Pin back; all-purpose cement

INSTRUCTIONS

Find center of chart and center of perforated paper; begin stitching there. Use three plies of floss or two strands of thread to work cross-stitches. Work blended needle as specified in key. Work backstitches using one ply of floss or two strands of thread. Use one strand of gold metallic thread to sew rocaille bead and heart sequin to end of Santa's chain.

Cover wrong side of stitchery with glue; center on felt and let dry. Trim one square beyond stitching as indicated on chart. Attach pin back with cement.

★★SNOWMAN PIN

As shown on page 83, finished snowman is 2⅛ inches tall.

MATERIALS

FABRICS
4x4-inch piece of 14-count gold perforated paper
2½x2½-inch piece of white felt

THREADS
Cotton embroidery floss in colors listed in key on page 92
Blending thread in colors listed in key on page 92
Metallic embroidery thread in color listed in key on page 92

SUPPLIES
Needle; red rocaille bead; crafts glue
Scissors
Two ¾-inch-long twigs
Pin back; all-purpose cement

INSTRUCTIONS

Find center of chart and of paper; begin stitching there. Use three plies of floss or two strands of thread to work cross-stitches. Work blended needle as specified in key. Work backstitches using one ply. Use one ply of garnet to sew bead to berries.

Cover wrong side of stitchery with glue; center on felt and let dry. Trim one square beyond stitched area of design as shown on chart.

Use three plies of golden brown (DMC 433) to sew on twig arms. Attach the pin back with cement.

★★ANGEL PIN

As shown on page 83, finished angel is 2 inches tall.

MATERIALS

FABRICS
4x4-inch piece of 14-count gold perforated paper
2½x2½-inch piece of white felt

THREADS
Cotton embroidery floss in colors listed in key on page 92
Blending thread in colors listed in key on page 92
Metallic embroidery thread in color listed in key on page 92

SUPPLIES
Needle
Six 3-millimeter gold beads
Red rocaille bead
¼-inch-diameter gold jump ring
½-inch-diameter gold star sequin
Crafts glue; scissors
Pin back; all-purpose cement

INSTRUCTIONS

Find center of chart and of paper; begin stitching there. Use three plies of floss or two strands of thread to work cross-stitches. Work blended needle as specified in key. Work backstitches using one ply of floss. *Do not* work holly berry on angel head at this time. Sew gold beads randomly to tree using one ply of green floss.

For hair, thread six plies of a short length of golden brown (DMC 433) in needle. From the front, insert needle in a hole at top of head. Bring needle to front through hole above first. Lay floss ends over face and top of head. Clip floss to about ½ inch and separate plies of floss. Work red holly berry cross-stitch over center of brown floss hair. Use one ply of red floss to sew rocaille bead to berries. Count six holes from left on bottom edge of skirt. Insert jump ring in hole; place star sequin on ring and pinch ring closed.

Cover wrong side of stitchery with glue; center on felt and let dry. Trim one square beyond stitching as indicated on chart. Attach pin back with cement.

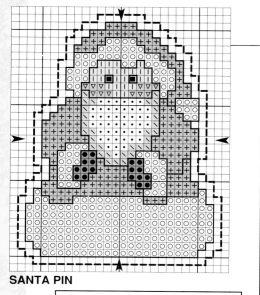

SANTA PIN

> *SANTA stitch count: 31 high x 24 wide*
> *SANTA finished design size:*
> *14-count fabric – 2¼ x 1¾ inches*

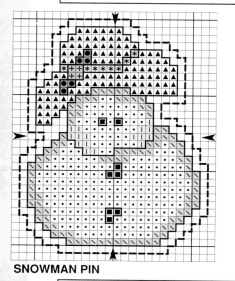

SNOWMAN PIN

> *SNOWMAN stitch count: 29 high x 22 wide*
> *SNOWMAN finished design size:*
> *14-count fabric – 2 x 1½ inches*

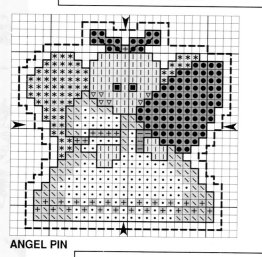

ANGEL PIN

> *ANGEL stitch count: 25 high x 25 wide*
> *ANGEL finished design size:*
> *14-count fabric – 1¾ x 1¾ inches*

SANTA, SNOWMAN, AND ANGEL PINS

ANCHOR		DMC	
002	·	000	White
403	■	310	Black
358	−	433	Golden brown
274	◣	928	Pale gray blue
1013	▽	3778	True terra cotta
868	I	3779	Pale terra cotta
	✳	282	Gold metallic thread

BLENDED NEEDLE

002	○	000	White (2X) and
		R306	Rainbow green blending thread (2X)
403	▲	310	Black (2X) and
		R617	Rainbow red blending thread (2X)
923	●	699	Christmas green (2X) and
		R306	Rainbow green blending thread (2X)
1005	+	816	Garnet (2X) and
		R617	Rainbow red blending thread (2X)

BACKSTITCH

	/	282	Gold metallic thread – chain to heart on santa
403	/	310	Black – all remaining stitches

★★TASSELED TREASURES NECKLACE

As shown on page 84.

MATERIALS
FABRIC
Two 3x3-inch pieces of 14-count white perforated paper or plastic
THREADS
#8 braid in colors listed in key
001 Kreinik silver #8 braid
SUPPLIES
Needle
Crafts glue

INSTRUCTIONS
Find center of chart and center of one piece of perforated paper; begin stitching there. Use one strand of braid to work cross-stitches and straight stitches. Trim stitchery one square beyond stitching. Repeat for remaining piece of perforated paper.

For cord, cut two 86-inch strands from *each* braid color, *including silver*. Combine cut lengths into a single strand. Secure one end of floss and twist; fold in half and allow to twist together. Overlap cords, 5 inches from each end; glue intersecting cords to center of wrong side of one necklace piece to form tassel.

To complete tassel, tie a 6-inch piece of thread around cord at edge of paper. Tie another 6-inch piece of thread around cord ¼ inch below the first knot. With edges of paper even, glue remaining stitchery to back of necklace over cord. Trim tassel ends.

★★TASSELED TREASURES EARRINGS

As shown on page 84.

MATERIALS
FABRIC
Four 3x3-inch pieces of 14-count white perforated paper or plastic
THREAD
#8 braid in colors listed in key
SUPPLIES
Needle
1¾x1¾-inch piece of cardboard
Two 1-inch pieces of .24-diameter wire
Two French ear wires
Needle-nose pliers
Crafts glue

INSTRUCTIONS
Find center of chart and center of one piece of perforated paper; begin stitching there. Use one strand of braid to work cross-stitches.

Trim finished stitchery one square beyond the stitched area. Repeat for remaining pieces of perforated paper.

For tassel, cut two 4-inch strands of braid; set aside. Wrap one strand of *each* braid color around cardboard twice. Thread 4-inch strand under braid at one edge of cardboard; tie. Cut bundle at opposite edge of cardboard; remove. Wrap remaining 4-inch strand of braid around bundle and tie. Glue ends of strand to bottom of earring.

Fold one piece of wire in half; insert through loop at bottom of one ear wire. Glue ends of wire to corner of earring opposite the tassel.

With edges of paper even, glue remaining stitchery to back of the first stitched piece. Trim tassel ends. Repeat for other earring.

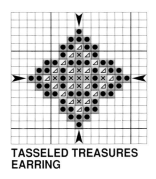

TASSELED TREASURES EARRING

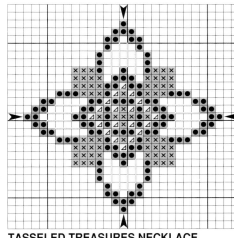

TASSELED TREASURES NECKLACE

***CHRISTMAS PARTY BUTTON COVERS AND EARRINGS

As shown on pages 84 and 85, each button cover and earring measures 1 inch in diameter.

MATERIALS
for each button cover or earring

FABRICS
5x5-inch piece of 25-count black Lugana fabric
3x3-inch piece of lightweight black fusible interfacing

THREADS
Cotton embroidery floss in colors listed in key on page 94
Metallic cord in color listed in key on page 94

SUPPLIES
Needle; embroidery hoop
⅞-inch-diameter button form
Button cover or earring back
Sewing thread
Wire cutters
All-purpose cement

INSTRUCTIONS
Tape or zigzag the edges of the Lugana fabric to prevent fraying. Find the center of chart and the center of fabric; begin stitching there.

Use one ply of floss or two strands of cord to work cross-stitches over *one thread* of fabric. Work back-stitches using two strands of cord.

Fuse the interfacing to the back of the stitched piece following the man-ufacturer's instructions. Center the design over the button form. Trim the fabric ½ inch beyond the edge.

Run a gathering thread ¼ inch from the cut edge. Pull up the gathers to smooth the fabric. Assemble the but-ton following the manufacturer's instructions.

Remove the button shank using wire cutters. Cement the button to the button cover or earring back. Repeat stitching and finishing instructions for other earring or for as many button covers as desired.

***CHRISTMAS PARTY CUMMERBUND

As shown on pages 84 and 85.

MATERIALS

FABRICS
8x19-inch piece of 25-count black Lugana fabric
8x19-inch piece of black faille
Two 8x19-inch pieces of medium-weight black fusible interfacing

THREADS
Cotton embroidery floss in colors listed in key on page 94
#8 braid in color listed in key on page 94
Metallic gold cord

SUPPLIES
Needle; embroidery hoop
2-millimeter gold torsade trim
Gold pailletes; tracing paper
Black sewing thread
1 yard of ⅝-inch-diameter black velvet cord
Tailor's chalk

TASSELED TREASURES JEWELRY
◿ 002 Kreinik metallic gold #8 braid
● 003 Kreinik metallic red #8 braid
☒ 008 Kreinik metallic green #8 braid
STRAIGHT STITCH
╱ 002 Kreinik metallic gold #8 braid
NECKLACE stitch count: 25 high x 25 wide
NECKLACE finished design size:
14-count fabric – 1¾ x 1¾ inches
EARRING stitch count: 13 high x 13 wide
EARRING finished design size:
14-count fabric – 1 x 1 inch

INSTRUCTIONS
Tape or zigzag the edges of the Lugana fabric to prevent fraying. Find the center of the chart and the center of the fabric; begin stitching there.

Use three plies of floss or one strand of braid to work cross-stitches over two threads of Lugana fabric. Use one strand of cord to couch torsade trim along scroll lines indicated on chart.

Sink the ends of the torsade trim to the wrong side of the stitched piece. Sew the gold pailletes to the stitched cummerbund using one strand of gold cord.

Fuse one piece of the interfacing to the wrong side of the stitchery following the manufacturer's instruc-tions. Fuse the remaining piece of interfacing to the faille.

Use the tailor's chalk to draw cummerbund outline as indicated on chart. Cut out ⅝ inches beyond out-line. Use cut piece as a pattern to cut one back from black faille. Sew pieces together using ⅝-inch seams with right sides facing unless other-wise specified.

Cut the velvet cord into two 18-inch pieces. Pin the ends of the cord between the layers of the cummerbund, with cord ends even with the centers of the cummerbund sides. Being careful to stitch through the ends of the cord and the cummer-bund only, sew the cummerbund closed; leave an opening at the bot-tom to turn.

Turn the cummerbund right side out and slip-stitch the opening closed. Knot the cord ends.

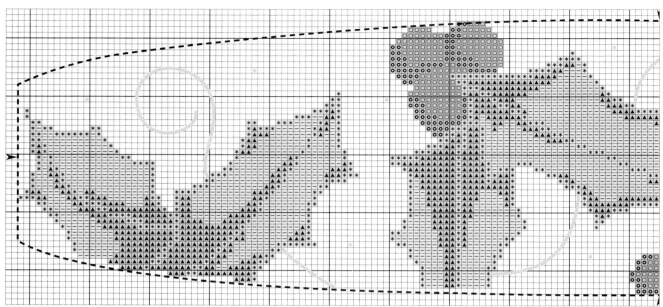

CHRISTMAS PARTY CUMMERBUND – LEFT

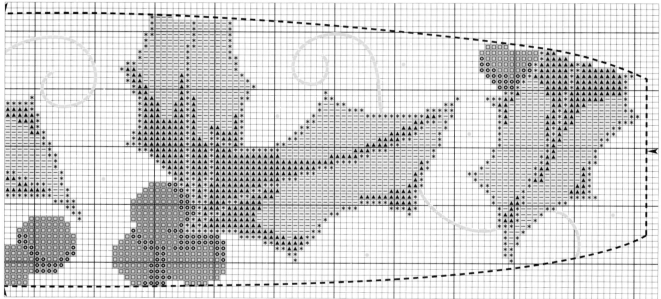

CHRISTMAS PARTY CUMMERBUND – RIGHT

CHRISTMAS PARTY CUMMERBUND

ANCHOR		DMC	
9046	⊙	321	Christmas red
046	◻	666	Red
923	▲	699	Dark Christmas green
226	−	702	Light Christmas green
	✳	002	Kreinik gold #8 fine braid

SEQUINS

   •   Gold #8 pailletes

VINES

         Kreinik 2mm gold torsade

Stitch count: 47 high x 213 wide

Finished design size:
14-count fabric – 3³⁄8 x 15¹⁄4 inches

CHRISTMAS PARTY BUTTON COVERS AND EARRINGS

ANCHOR		DMC	
9046	⊙	321	Christmas red
923	▲	699	Dark Christmas green
226	−	702	Light Christmas green
	✳	002	Kreinik gold cord

BACKSTITCH

   ╱   002 Kreinik gold cord

Stitch count: 22 high x 19 wide

Finished design size:
14-count fabric – 1¹⁄2 x 1³⁄8 inches

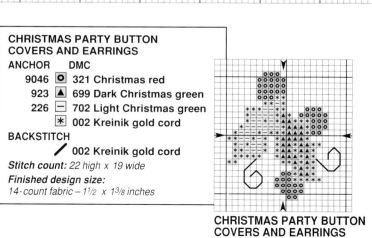

CHRISTMAS PARTY BUTTON COVERS AND EARRINGS

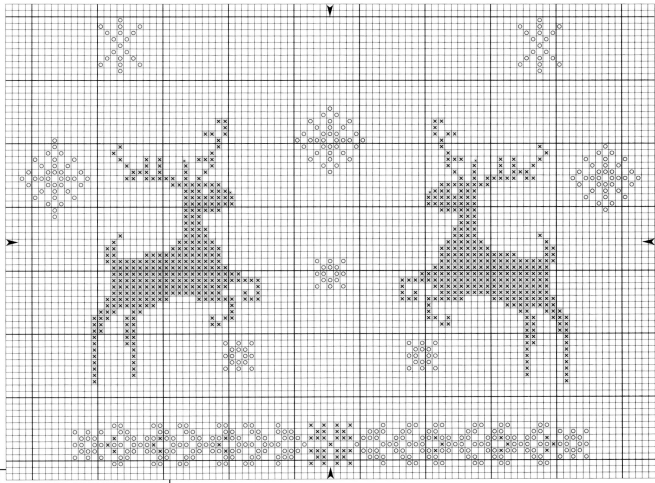

REINDEER SWEATER

ANCHOR		DMC	
387	○		Ecru
1008	✕	3773	Rose beige

Stitch count: 71 high x 95 wide

Finished design sizes:
As pictured – 7¹/₈ x 13¹/₈ inches
8¹/₂-count fabric – 8³/₈ x 11¹/₈ inches
14-count fabric – 5 x 6³/₄ inches

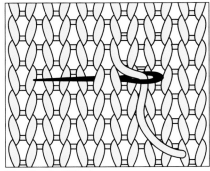

Duplicate Stitch

★★REINDEER SWEATER

As shown on page 86, duplicate-stitch design measures 7¹/₈x13¹/₈ inches.

MATERIALS
FABRIC
Purchased blue crew neck sweater with a gauge of 7 stitches and 10 rows = 1 inch
FLOSS
Cotton embroidery floss in colors listed in key
SUPPLIES
Tapestry needle; measuring tape

INSTRUCTIONS
Wash sweater and allow it to dry. Find the vertical center of the sweater front. Sew a line of basting stitches from top to bottom of sweater.

Measure along the basting to a point 2 inches below the lower edge of the neckband ribbing; and begin stitching top of the center snowflake there. Use six plies of floss to work duplicate stitches.

★★SWEETHEART HOLIDAY COLLAR

As shown on page 87.

MATERIALS
FABRIC
Purchased small 28-count Irish linen collar
FLOSS
Cotton embroidery floss in colors listed in key on page 96
SUPPLIES
Needle
Three ³/₈-inch-wide heart-shaped buttons
White sewing thread

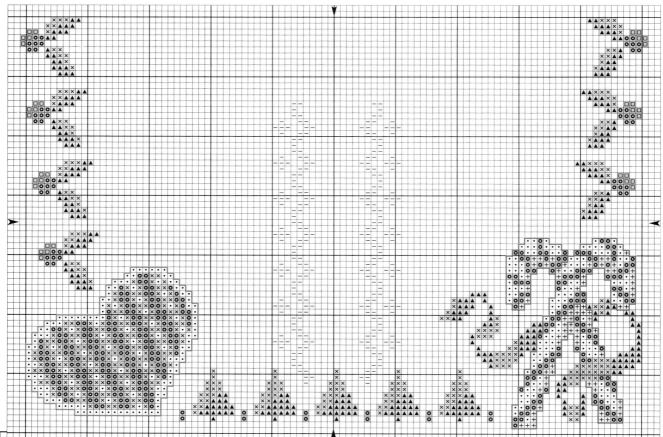

SWEETHEART HOLIDAY COLLAR

ANCHOR		DMC	
387	−		Ecru
002	•	000	White
046	◉	666	Red
1021	+	761	Salmon
230	▲	909	Deep emerald
205	✕	911	Medium emerald
035	▢	3705	Watermelon
BACKSTITCH			
9046	╱	321	Christmas red – all stitches

Stitch count: 69 high x 102 wide
Finished design size:
14-count fabric – 5 x 7¼ inches

INSTRUCTIONS

Find top stitch in center tree motif on chart and vertical center of collar. Begin stitching tree motif 1 inch from bottom edge of collar.

Use three plies of floss to work cross-stitches over two threads of fabric. Work backstitches using one ply of floss.

Press collar from the back. Sew buttons to collar. Slip-stitch opening closed.

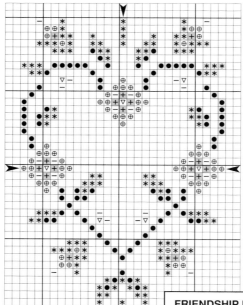

FRIENDSHIP MITTENS

FRIENDSHIP MITTENS
RIBBONFLOSS

●	142F-9	Grass green
+	142F-12	Red
▽	142F-17	Honey
−	142F-25	Soft yellow
⊕	144F-2	Metallic silver
✳	144F-6	Metallic green

Stitch count: 41 high x 27 wide
Finished design sizes:
As pictured – 3½ x 3⅛ inches

★★FRIENDSHIP MITTENS

As shown on page 88.

MATERIALS
FABRIC
Purchased red mittens with a gauge of 9 stitches and 12 rows = 1 inch
FLOSS
Ribbonfloss braided ribbon in colors listed in key
SUPPLIES
Tapestry needle; measuring tape

INSTRUCTIONS

Find the vertical center of the chart and one mitten back. With cuff at the bottom, measure to a point 2 inches above the ribbing; begin stitching bottom of the motif there. Use one strand of braided ribbon to work all duplicate stitches. Repeat for the remaining mitten.

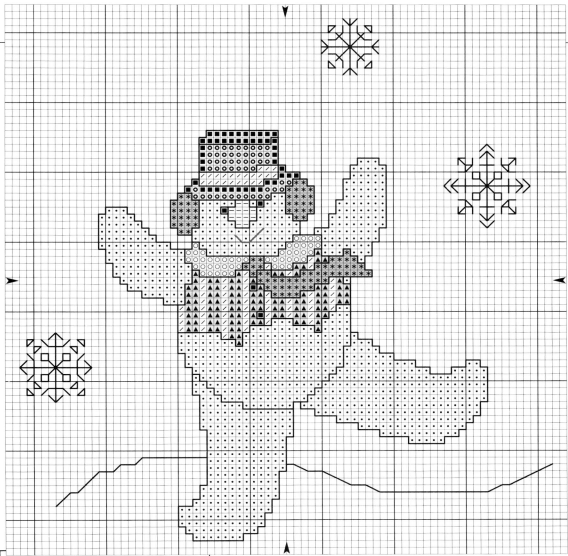

SNOWMAN SWEATSHIRT

ANCHOR		DMC	
002	·	000	White
403	■	310	Black
9046	✳	321	Christmas red
923	▲	699	Christmas green
271	–	819	Pink
206	○	955	Nile green
292	╱	3078	Lemon
236	◉	3799	Charcoal

BACKSTITCH

002	╱	000	White – snowflakes, snow line
403	╱	310	Black – snowman
9046	╱	321	Christmas red – mouth

Stitch count: 75 high x 74 wide

Finished design sizes:
8½-count fabric – 8⅞ x 8¾ inches
6½-count fabric –11½ x 11⅜ inches
11-count fabric – 6⅞ x 6¾ inches

**SNOWMAN SHIRT

As shown on page 89.

MATERIALS
FABRICS
Purchased red sweatshirt
12x12-inch piece of 8½-count waste canvas
12x12-inch piece of lightweight fusible interfacing
FLOSS
Cotton embroidery floss in colors listed in key
SUPPLIES
Needle
Measuring tape
Basting thread; tweezers

INSTRUCTIONS
Wash and dry sweatshirt. Tape or zigzag edges of waste canvas to prevent fraying. Baste waste canvas on front of sweatshirt, centering left to right, with top edge of canvas at bottom of neckband.

Find vertical center of chart and vertical center of canvas. Measure 3 inches from bottom of neckband ribbing; begin stitching the right stitch in the top row of hat there.

Use six plies of floss to work cross-stitches. Work backstitches using two plies of floss.

Remove the basting threads and trim the waste canvas close to the stitching. Wet the waste canvas and, using the tweezers, pull the individual waste canvas threads from under the cross-stitches.

Fuse the lightweight interfacing over the stitching on the inside of the sweatshirt following the manufacturer's instructions.

All Through the House

Bring the warmth of the holidays into your home by filling it with your own cross-stitched works of art. In this chapter you'll discover glorious pieces to deck your walls, trims to proudly hang on your tree, and a quilt to cuddle under when a hush falls over your holiday home. We hope this fabulous collection inspires you to create the best-dressed Christmas home ever—a spectacular holiday haven that makes even a simple glass of sparkling cider taste extra special.

Tidings of Joy Sampler, Tree Base, Place Mat, Place Cards, and Ornaments

Exquisite stitches and glittering metallic threads are used to create this lovely sampler destined to become an heirloom. For a smaller, but equally elegant project, work the specialty stitch trees on a band of fabric to make a miniature tree container. Or, stitch the snowflake motifs as ornaments or accessories for your holiday table. Instructions and chart begin on page 104.

DESIGNER: MARY B. JONES ● PHOTOGRAPHERS: OPPOSITE, SCOTT LITTLE; ABOVE, HOPKINS ASSOCIATES

Santa's Wish Sampler

Extend a jolly welcome to all this year by stitching this delightful Santa sampler. Worked on dark blue Aida cloth in cotton floss and metallic gold threads, this piece comes to life with accents of shiny gold French knots on the tree and backstitches that bring out the details on cheery St. Nick. Instructions and chart are on page 109.

DESIGNER: HELEN NICHOLSON ● PHOTOGRAPHER: SCOTT LITTLE

Christmas Music Bellpull

The familiar strains of a favorite Christmas carol were the inspiration for this bellpull design. The musical score accompanies the cross-stitched illustrations of the first five verses. Worked on 14-count white Aida cloth and trimmed in bright plaid, this charming bellpull is a striking accent for any room. Instructions and chart are on pages 110–111.

DESIGNER: CAROLE RODGERS ● PHOTOGRAPHER: SCOTT LITTLE

Noah's Ark Quilt, Ornaments, and Tree Topper

"And Noah built an ark, and two-by-two, the animals came." The figures from this favorite Biblical story are recreated here in colorful cross-stitch. Worked on 14-count Aida cloth and trimmed with braid, the ark and animals bring a special charm to this Christmas tree. Stitch the same motifs on 8-count Aida, sew them together, and spend Christmas morning snuggled under the soft comfort of this clever quilt. For a festive finish, we've framed each of the rectangles in bold-colored ribbons. Instructions and charts begin on page 111.

DESIGNER: JIM WILLIAMS ● PHOTOGRAPHER: SCOTT LITTLE

★★★★TIDINGS OF JOY SAMPLER

As shown on page 99.

MATERIALS
FABRIC
15x21-inch piece of 28-count antique ivory Jobelan fabric
THREADS
Cotton embroidery floss in colors listed in key on page 108
Flower thread in colors listed in key on page 108
#8 and #16 braid in colors listed in key on page 108
SUPPLIES
Embroidery hoop
Needle
Seed beads in color listed in key on page 108
Desired mat
Desired frame

INSTRUCTIONS
Tape or zigzag the edges of the fabric to prevent fraying. Find center of chart and center of fabric; begin stitching there.

Use two plies of floss to work cross-stitches over two threads of fabric. Work backstitches using one ply of floss or one strand of flower thread or braid. Work blended needle as specified in key. Work French knots as specified in key.

For each section of the design, work all of the cross-stitches before the specialty stitches. Referring to the diagrams, *opposite,* work the diamond eye stitches, Smyrna cross stitches, oblong crosses with backstitch, vertical satin stitches, Florentine stitches, double herringbone stitches, and rice stitches using two plies of floss or one strand of flower thread. Use one strand of flower thread to couch gold braid borders. Use the alphabet, *page 108,* to stitch initials and to change the year if needed.

Press the finished stitchery from the back using a press cloth. Mat and frame piece as desired.

★★TIDINGS OF JOY PLACE MAT

As shown on page 98.

MATERIALS *for each mat*
FABRIC
Purchased 12x18-inch 28-count gold and cream Silvretta place mat
THREADS
Cotton embroidery floss in colors listed in key on page 108
Blending filament in colors listed in key on page 108
SUPPLIES
Needle

INSTRUCTIONS
Find center of desired snowflake motif, *pages 106–107,* and center of one corner square of place mat. Begin stitching there. Work cross-stitches using blended needle as specified in key. Stitch a snowflake motif in each corner of place mat. Press from back.

★★TIDINGS OF JOY PLACE CARDS

As shown on page 98, finished place cards are 1½x3¾ inches.

MATERIALS *for each card*
FABRICS
3x3-inch piece of 14-count red perforated paper
3x3¾-inch purchased white place card
THREADS
Cotton embroidery floss in colors listed in key on page 108
Blending filament in colors listed in key on page 108
SUPPLIES
Needle; crafts glue; calligraphy pen

INSTRUCTIONS
Find the center of the desired snowflake motif, *pages 106–107,* and the center of one piece of paper; begin stitching there. Work cross-stitches with blended needle as specified in the key.

Trim paper one square beyond the stitched area of design. Position and glue snowflake motif on left side of place card. Using pen, write desired name on card.

★★★★TIDINGS OF JOY TREE BASE

As shown on page 98.

MATERIALS
FABRICS
7x18-inch piece of 28-count antique ivory Jobelan fabric
3½x14½-inch piece of fleece
4-inch-diameter felt circle
THREADS
Cotton embroidery floss in colors listed in key on page 108
Flower thread in colors listed in key on page 108
SUPPLIES
Embroidery hoop
Needle
3½-inch-tall and 4-inch-diameter round container
Crafts glue
15-inch piece of ¾-inch-wide burgundy and gold flat lace
15-inch piece of ½-inch-wide metallic gold and green flat braid trim
One yard of metallic gold cord

INSTRUCTIONS
Tape or zigzag edges of Jobelan fabric to prevent fraying. Find the center of tree band on chart, *pages 106–107,* and the center of fabric; begin stitching there.

Use two plies of floss to work cross-stitches over two threads of fabric. Work backstitches using one strand of flower thread. Work blended needle as specified in key.

Refer to the diagrams, *opposite,* to work oblong crosses with backstitch, vertical satin stitches, Florentine stitches, double herringbone stitches, and rice stitches using two plies of floss or one strand of flower thread. Press the finished stitchery from the back.

Glue fleece around container. Centering design, trim Jobelan to 5½x15 inches. Fold one end of Jobelan under 1 inch. Centering design top to bottom, glue stitchery around container overlapping edges at back. Fold excess fabric to inside and bottom of container; glue.

Glue lace around top edge of container. Glue remaining trim around bottom edge of container. Glue felt to bottom of container. Tie gold cord around container top and tie in a bow.

★★TIDINGS OF JOY ORNAMENTS

As shown on page 98, finished ornaments are 4 inches tall, including tassels.

MATERIALS
for each ornament
FABRICS
3x3-inch piece of 14-count red or gold perforated paper
3x3-inch piece of red or gold card stock
THREADS
Cotton embroidery floss in colors listed in key on page 108
Blending filaments in colors listed in key on page 108
#8 metallic braid as listed in key on page 108
SUPPLIES
Needle
1¾-inch piece of cardboard
Crafts glue

INSTRUCTIONS
Find center of desired snowflake motif, *pages 106–107,* and of perforated paper; begin stitching there.

Work cross-stitches with blended needle as specified in key. Trim paper one square beyond the stitched area of design.

For tassel, cut two 6-inch strands of braid; set aside. Wrap one strand of braid from spool around cardboard 24 times. Thread one 6-inch strand under thread at one edge of cardboard; tie. Cut thread at opposite

edge; remove. Wrap remaining 6-inch strand of thread around the bundle and tie. Glue ends of first 6-inch strand to the bottom point of the perforated paper snowflake.

For hanger, cut a 6-inch piece of braid. Fold braid in half. Glue the cut ends of the braid at top point of the perforated paper snowflake.

Glue card stock to back of stitchery. Trim even with stitched piece.

① **Diamond Eye Stitch**

② **Couching**

③ **Smyrna Cross Stitch**

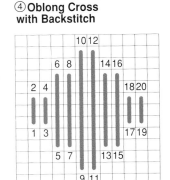

④**Oblong Cross with Backstitch**

⑤ **Vertical Satin Stitch**

⑥ **Florentine Stitch**

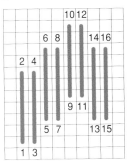

⑦**Double Herringbone (first journey)**

Double Herringbone (second journey)

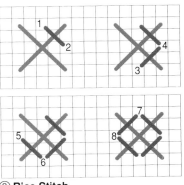

⑧ **Rice Stitch**

TIDINGS OF JOY SAMPLER, PLACE MAT, PLACE CARDS, TREE BASE, AND ORNAMENTS

TIDINGS OF JOY SAMPLER, PLACE MAT, PLACE CARDS, TREE BASE, AND ORNAMENTS

ANCHOR		DMC	
218	●	319	Dark pistachio
215	▽	320	True pistachio
217	✕	367	Medium pistachio
214	−	368	Light pistachio
045	▲	814	Dark garnet
043	◉	815	Medium garnet

BLENDED NEEDLE

218	◉	319	Dark pistachio (2X) and
		008	Kreinik green blending filament (1X)
1005	▢	498	Christmas red (2X) and
		003	Kreinik red blending filament (1X)
891	✳	676	Light old gold (1X) and
		002	Kreinik gold blending filament (2X)

BACKSTITCH

1005	╱	498	Christmas red— large poinsettias
891	╱	676	Light old gold— side borders
890	╱	729	Medium old gold— all outside borders, borders around numbers
045	╱	814	Dark garnet— lower row of zigzag
043	╱	815	Medium garnet— small poinsettias, upper row of zigzag
	╱	2320	True pistachio flower thread—name and date
	╱	2815	Medium garnet flower thread—saying, corner snowflakes
	╱	2890	Hunter green flower thread—tree 7
	╱	002	Kreinik gold #8 braid— borders around alphabet letters

STRAIGHT STITCH

	▎	2890	Hunter green flower thread—centers of tree 7

BLENDED BACKSTITCH

926	╱	712	Cream (1X) and
		002	Kreinik gold blending filament (2X)— alphabet background

FRENCH KNOT

	●	2815	Medium garnet flower thread—holly berries (3 wraps), dots over "i"s and "j" (1 wrap)

SEED BEADS

	●	00557	Mill Hill gold seed bead

DIAMOND EYE STITCH

890	✳	729	Medium old gold— upper border

ANCHOR		DMC	
COUCHING			
	━	002	Kreinik gold #16 braid— borders
	✕	2815	Medium garnet flower thread
	✕	2890	Hunter green flower thread

SMYRNA CROSS STITCH

387	✳		Ecru

OBLONG CROSS WITH BACKSTITCH

	✖	2319	Dark pistachio flower thread

VERTICAL SATIN STITCH

	▎	2319	Dark pistachio flower thread
	▎	2320	True pistachio flower thread
	▎	2369	Light pistachio flower thread
	▎	2890	Hunter green flower thread

FLORENTINE STITCH

	▎	2319	Dark pistachio flower thread
	▎	2320	True pistachio flower thread
	▎	2369	Light pistachio flower thread
	▎	2890	Hunter green flower thread

DOUBLE HERRINGBONE STITCH

218	✕	890	Deep pistachio— first journey
217	✕	367	Medium pistachio— second journey

RICE STITCH

	✕	2319	Dark pistachio flower thread— first journey
	◇	2815	Medium garnet flower thread— second journey

SAMPLER stitch count: 132 high x 208 wide

SAMPLER finished design sizes:
14-count fabric – 9³⁄₈ x 14⁷⁄₈ inches
12¹⁄₂-count fabric –10¹⁄₂ x 16⁵⁄₈ inches
16-count fabric – 8¹⁄₄ x 13 inches

TREE BASE stitch count: 26 high x 171 wide

TREE BASE finished design sizes:
14-count fabric –1⁷⁄₈ x 12¹⁄₄ inches
12¹⁄₂-count fabric – 2 x 13⁵⁄₈ inches
16-count fabric – 1⁵⁄₈ x 10⁵⁄₈ inches

SNOWFLAKE MOTIF stitch count:
(ornament, place card, place mat)
15 high x 15 wide

SNOWFLAKE MOTIF finished design sizes:
14-count fabric – 1 x 1 inch
12¹⁄₂-count fabric –1¹⁄₈ x 1¹⁄₈ inches
16-count fabric – ⁷⁄₈ x ⁷⁄₈ inch

TIDINGS OF JOY ALPHABET

★★SANTA'S WISH SAMPLER

As shown on page 100.

MATERIALS

FABRIC

10x16-inch piece of 14-count dark blue Aida cloth

THREADS

Cotton embroidery floss in colors listed in key

Metallic gold embroidery thread as listed in key

SUPPLIES

Needle

Embroidery hoop

Desired frame and mat

INSTRUCTIONS

Tape or zigzag the edges of fabric to prevent fraying. Find center of chart and center of fabric; begin stitching there.

Use two plies of floss to work cross-stitches. Work backstitches, French knots, and straight stitches using one ply of floss or one strand of metallic gold thread.

Press finished stitchery from the back. Mat and frame as desired.

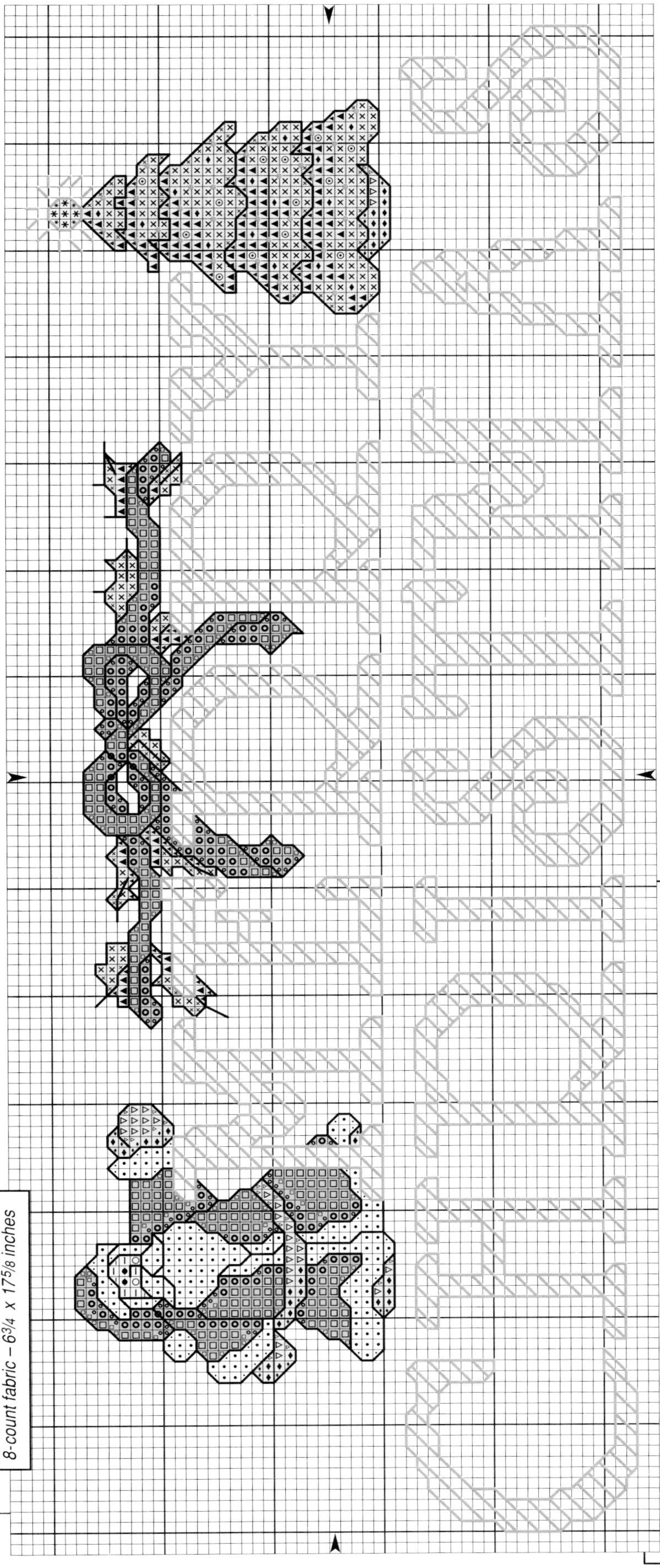

Stitch count: *54 high x 141 wide*

Finished design sizes:

14-count fabric – 3 7/8 x 10 inches

11-count fabric – 5 x 12 3/4 inches

8-count fabric – 6 3/4 x 17 5/8 inches

SANTA'S WISH SAMPLER

ANCHOR		DMC
002	•	000 White
1006	◉	304 Medium Christmas red
9046	▣	321 True Christmas red
009	○	352 Coral
008	|	353 Peach
358	♦	433 Deep golden brown
1046	▷	435 True golden brown
228	×	700 Christmas green
136	◎	799 Delft blue
230	◀	909 Emerald
	✳	282 Gold metallic thread

ANCHOR		DMC
BACKSTITCH		
403	/	310 Black – Santa, tree, ribbon, leaves
	/	282 Gold metallic thread – lettering, star
STRAIGHT STITCH		
	/	282 Gold metallic thread – star burst
FRENCH KNOT		
403	•	310 Black – Santa's eyes
	•	282 Gold metallic thread – tree trim

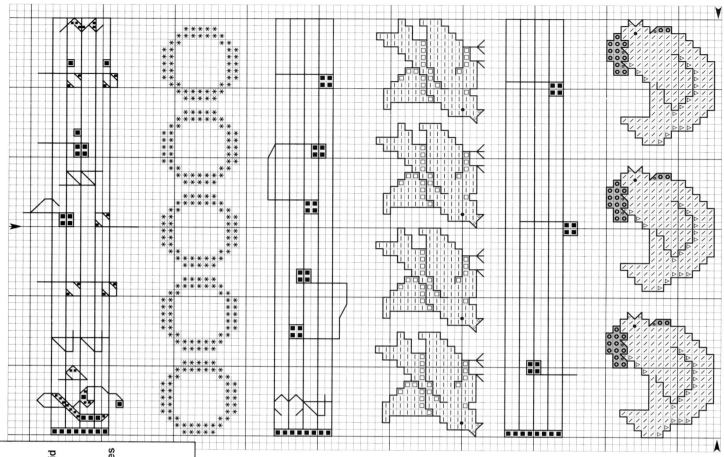

ANCHOR	DMC	
	378	841 True beige brown
	388	842 Light beige brown
		002 Kreinik gold #8 braid

CHRISTMAS MUSIC BELLPULL

ANCHOR	DMC	
002	000	White
403	310	Black
9046	321	Christmas red
398	415	Pearl gray
310	434	Golden brown
923	699	Dark Christmas green
228	700	Medium Christmas green
295	726	Topaz
301	744	Medium yellow
300	745	Light yellow
359	801	Coffee brown

BACKSTITCH
403 / 310 Black–all stitches

FRENCH KNOT
403 • 310 Black–all birds' eyes

Stitch count: 193 high x 60 wide
Finished design sizes:
14-count fabric – 13³⁄₄ x 4¹⁄₄ inches
11-count fabric – 17¹⁄₂ x 5¹⁄₂ inches
8-count fabric – 24¹⁄₄ x 7¹⁄₂ inches

★★CHRISTMAS MUSIC BELLPULL

As shown on page 101, finished bellpull is 15x5¹⁄₂ inches without the hardware.

MATERIALS
FABRICS
10x20-inch piece of 14-count white Aida cloth
10x20-inch piece of lightweight fusible interfacing
¹⁄₃ yard of 45-inch-wide red and green plaid taffeta
THREADS
Cotton embroidery floss in colors listed in key
#8 braid in color listed in key
SUPPLIES
Needle
Embroidery hoop
Sewing thread
Two 16¹⁄₂-inch pieces of cording
6³⁄₈-inch-wide bellpull hardware

INSTRUCTIONS
Tape or zigzag the edges of the Aida cloth to prevent fraying. Find the center of chart and the center of fabric; begin stitching there. Use three plies of floss or one strand of braid to work cross-stitches. Work French knots using one ply of floss. Work backstitches using two plies of floss.

Centering design, fuse the lightweight interfacing to the wrong side of the stitchery following the manufacturer's instructions. Trim the fabric to 16¹⁄₂x5¹⁄₂ inches. All seams are sewn with right sides together in ¹⁄₄-inch seams unless otherwise specified.

From plaid fabric, cut one 16¹⁄₂x5¹⁄₂-inch bellpull back, and two 1¹⁄₂x16¹⁄₂-inch bias piping strips. Center cording lengthwise on wrong side of piping strips. Fold fabric around cording, raw edges together. Use a zipper foot to sew through both layers close to stitching. Sew one

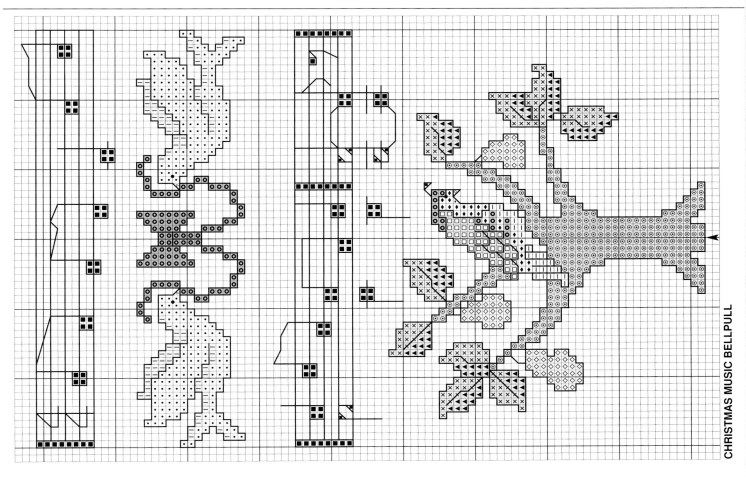

piece of covered cording to each long side of bellpull, raw edges even.

Sew front to back with the right sides facing, leaving an opening at the top for turning. Trim seams, turn, and press. Insert the ends of the bellpull through bellpull hardware from the front. Fold ½ inch to the back and whipstitch fabric ends to back of bellpull.

✶✶NOAH'S ARK ORNAMENTS

As shown on page 102–103, finished ornaments measure from 3¼x5¼ to 5½x6½ inches tall.

MATERIALS
for each ornament
FABRICS
8x10-inch piece of 14-count ivory Aida cloth
6x8-inch piece of green felt

FLOSS
Cotton embroidery floss in colors listed in key on page 113
SUPPLIES
Needle; embroidery hoop
Erasable marker
Tracing paper
Pencil
6x8-inch piece of self-stick mounting board with foam
One or two 24-inch pieces of ⅜-inch to ½-inch-wide flat braid trim
24-inch piece of ½-inch-wide gold metallic ribbon
Crafts glue

INSTRUCTIONS
Tape or zigzag the edges of the Aida cloth to prevent fraying. Find the center of the desired animal chart and the center of Aida cloth; begin stitching there.

Use three plies of floss to work cross-stitches. Work backstitches using one ply of floss. Work French knots using two plies of floss.

Use the erasable marker to draw a simplified shape ½ inch beyond the outline of the stitched design. Cut out the Aida cloth ½ inch beyond the marker line.

Lay tracing paper on fabric and trace marker line with pencil; cut out. Use the paper pattern to cut shape from mounting board and felt.

Peel the protective paper from the mounting board. Center the foam side of the mounting board on the back of the stitched design and press to stick. Fold the raw edges of Aida cloth to the back and glue.

Beginning at the bottom of the figure, glue one row of braid around the edge of the ornament. Glue a second row of braid around the ornament, if desired.

Fold the metallic ribbon in half. Glue folded edge of ribbon to the top edge of the ornament. Tie the ends of the ribbon into a bow to make the hanging loop. Glue the felt to the back of ornament.

**NOAH'S ARK TREE TOPPER

As shown on page 103, tree topper measures 9½x8 inches.

MATERIALS
FABRICS
15x12-inch piece of 14-count ivory Aida cloth

15x12-inch piece of fleece

15x12-inch piece of lightweight fusible interfacing

15x12-inch piece of red print cotton fabric

FLOSS
Cotton embroidery floss in colors listed in key

SUPPLIES
Needle

Embroidery hoop

1 yard of ¾-inch-wide braid trim

Two 10½x13½-inch sheets of plastic canvas

One yard of gold metallic piping

Crafts glue

Tissue paper

Pencil

INSTRUCTIONS

Tape or zigzag the edges of the Aida cloth to prevent fraying. Find the center of the chart and the center of the Aida cloth; begin stitching there.

Use three plies of floss to work cross-stitches. Work French knots using two plies of floss. Use one ply of black floss to work backstitches. All seams are sewn with right sides together in ¼-inch seams unless otherwise specified.

With wrong sides together, baste the finished cross-stitched piece and the fleece rectangles together ¼ inch beyond the stitched area of the design. Curve the basting line around the design to simplify the shape. Trim the stitchery ¼ inch beyond the basting line. Sew gold piping to the ark front along the basting line with raw edges even.

Fuse the lightweight interfacing to the back of the red fabric following

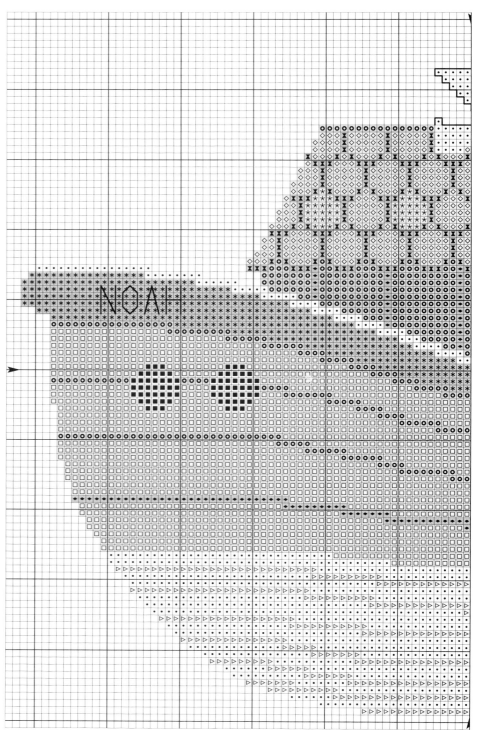

ARK

manufacturer's instructions. Use Aida cloth as a pattern to cut a back from red fabric.

Sew the front and back of the ark together, leaving a 5½-inch-long opening at the bottom center. Trim the seams and turn right side out.

Press the opening seam allowances to the inside.

Using the ark as a pattern, cut a front and a back from the plastic canvas. Trim the plastic ⅛ inch smaller than the traced outline of the ark. Roll the plastic and insert the shapes

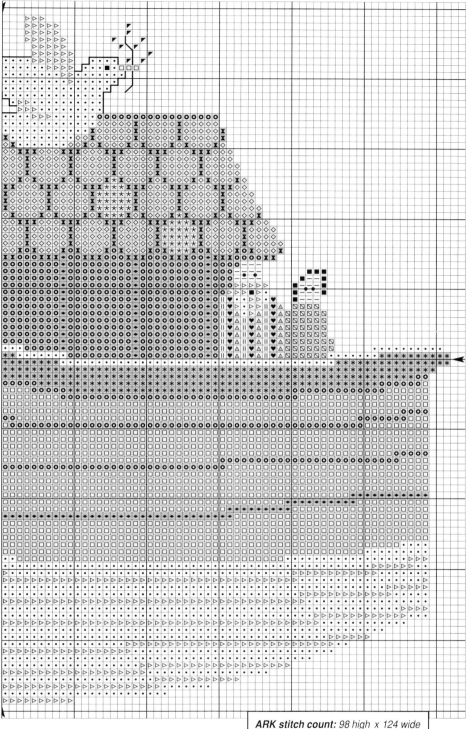

ARK stitch count: 98 high x 124 wide
ARK finished design sizes:
8-count fabric – 12¼ x 15½ inches
14-count fabric – 7⅝ x 8⅞ inches

NOAH'S ARK ORNAMENTS, TREE TOPPER, AND QUILT

ANCHOR		DMC	
002	·	000	White
403	■	310	Black
215	◪	320	True pistachio
9046	✳	321	Christmas red
008	♡	353	Peach
217	⊞	367	Medium pistachio
1047	◌	402	Mahogany
401	●	413	Pewter
235	♯	414	Steel
398	▽	415	Light pearl gray
310	✕	434	Medium golden brown
266	☆	471	Avocado
683	◼	500	Blue green
098	△	553	Violet
281	❖	580	Moss green
901	⊙	680	Dark old gold
088	◆	718	Light plum
295	‖	726	Topaz
890	◿	729	Medium old gold
845	▲	730	Olive
275	╲	746	Off white
234	▷	762	Pale pearl gray
359	★	801	Medium coffee brown
168	◨	807	Peacock blue
277	✲	830	Dark bronze
907	▣	832	Medium bronze
945	╱	833	Light bronze
218	⋈	890	Deep pistachio
360	◆	898	Dark coffee brown
256	◤	906	Parrot green
1029	♥	915	Dark plum
1014	◯	919	Red copper
1003	▽	922	Copper
848	◈	927	Gray blue
881	−	945	Dark ivory
1010	⎮	951	Medium ivory
1001	◌	976	Light golden brown
1002	▢	977	Pale golden brown
187	◇	992	Medium aquamarine
186	✳	993	Light aquamarine
410	▦	995	Dark electric blue
433	⊕	996	Medium electric blue
397	＋	3024	Brown gray
391	◿	3033	Mocha
888	＝	3045	Yellow beige

BACKSTITCH

890	╱	729	Medium old gold – giraffe
403	╱	310	Black – all remaining stitches

FRENCH KNOT

403	●	310	Black – eyes
088	·	718	Light plum – peacock
845	·	730	Olive – peahen

into the tree topper, pushing one against the front and one against the back. Tack the bottom of the plastic canvas pieces to the seam allowance of the ark opening to secure. Glue the trim around the outside edge of ark behind the piping.

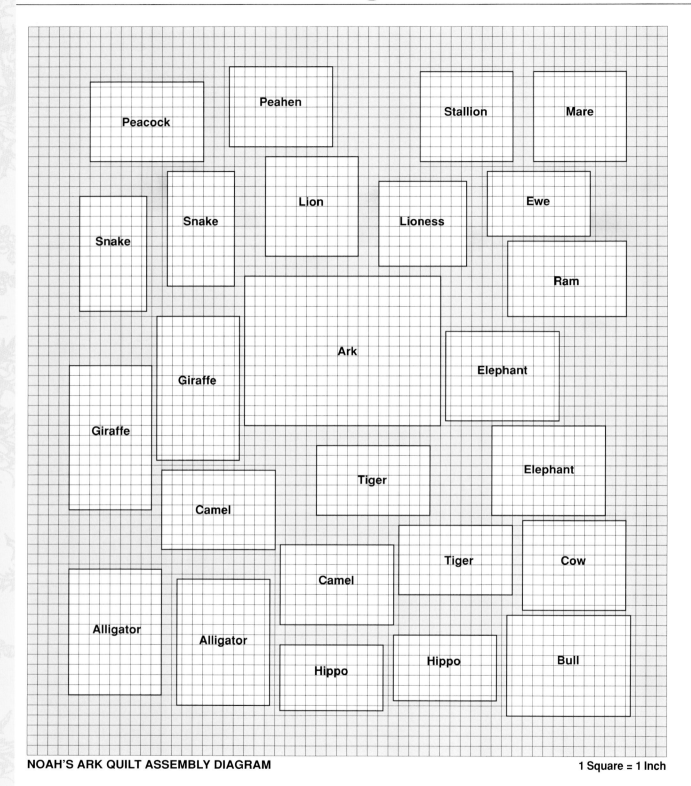

NOAH'S ARK QUILT ASSEMBLY DIAGRAM

1 Square = 1 Inch

**NOAH'S ARK QUILT

As shown on pages 102–103, finished quilt measures 73x62 inches.

MATERIALS

FABRICS

4⅔ yards of 42-inch-wide 8-count beige Aida cloth

4¼ yards of 45-inch-wide red print cotton fabric

Two yards of 60-inch-wide green and white check fabric

73x62-inch piece of quilt batting

FLOSS

Cotton embroidery floss in colors listed in key on page 113

SUPPLIES

Needle

Embroidery hoop

Seven yards of ⅝-inch-wide royal blue grosgrain ribbon (elephant, hippo, and peacock trim)

5⅛ yards of ⅞-inch-wide maroon grosgrain ribbon (cow and lion trim)

4¾ yards of ⅝-inch-wide red grosgrain ribbon (camel and horse trim)

4½ yards of ⅝-inch-wide orange grosgrain ribbon (tiger and sheep trim)

2⅞ yards of ⅞-inch-wide salmon grosgrain ribbon (giraffe trim)

4⅔ yards of ⅞-inch-wide green grosgrain ribbon (alligator and ark trim)

2¼ yards of ⅝-inch-wide rust grosgrain ribbon (snake trim)

Two yards of ⅞-inch-wide turquoise grosgrain ribbon (ark trim)

Two yards of 1-inch-wide green grosgrain ribbon (ark trim)

Sewing threads to match fabrics and ribbons

Eight yards of ⅞-inch-wide royal blue grosgrain ribbon (quilt border)

INSTRUCTIONS

From Aida cloth, cut two 10x12-inch pieces for peacocks; four 14x10-inch pieces for snakes and tigers; six 12x14-inch pieces for camels, alligators, bull, and ram; two 18x10-inch pieces for giraffes; one 18x21-inch piece for ark; and ten

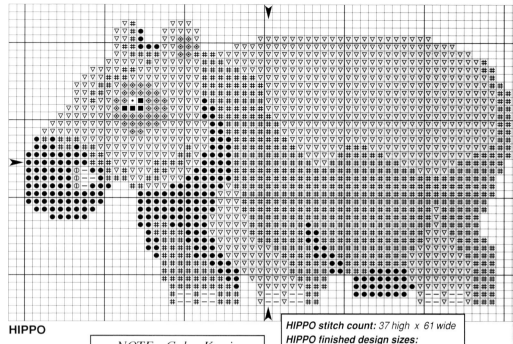

HIPPO

NOTE: Color Key is on page 113.

HIPPO stitch count: *37 high x 61 wide*
HIPPO finished design sizes:
8-count fabric – 4⅝ x 7⅝ inches
14-count fabric – 2⅝ x 4⅜ inches

12x12-inch pieces for *each* of the remaining animals.

Tape or zigzag the edges of Aida cloth to prevent fraying. Find the center of desired chart and the center of corresponding fabric piece; begin stitching there.

Use four plies of floss to work cross-stitches. Work backstitches using three plies. Use two plies of floss for the French knots.

Trim each stitched piece in a rectangle 1 inch beyond the stitched area. All measurements include ½-inch seam allowance. Sew seams with right sides facing unless otherwise specified. With grosgrain ribbon overlapping Aida cloth edges ¼ inch, topstitch the appropriate ribbon around front of each piece, mitering the corners.

For the ark, first topstitch turquoise ribbon to the Aida cloth edges. Sew the edges of the green ribbon to the outer edge of the turquoise ribbon, with the green ribbon overlapping the turquoise ribbon ½ inch. Press all stitched pieces from back if desired.

From red fabric, cut two 31x71-inch pieces. Join long edges to make

a 60x71-inch quilt top. Also cut two 74x5-inch and two 63x5-inch binding strips from red fabric.

Referring to the quilt assembly diagram, *opposite,* baste the animal and ark blocks onto the quilt top. Topstitch the pieces in place, stitching close to the outer edge of the ribbon. Remove the basting threads.

Layer the green and white fabric, batting, and quilt top. Baste the layers together, working from the center outward in a spoke pattern. Machine-quilt around the ark and the animal rectangles.

To bind the quilt, with the right sides of the binding and the quilt back together, sew the longer strips to long sides and the shorter strips to short sides through all layers. Trim excess fabric and miter the corners. Turn the strips to the front, miter corners, and turn under ½ inch along the raw edges.

Topstitch the binding to the quilt front. Sew the wide royal blue grosgrain ribbon around the quilt just inside the binding.

Topstitch along each edge of ribbon, mitering the corners. Remove the basting.

All Through the House

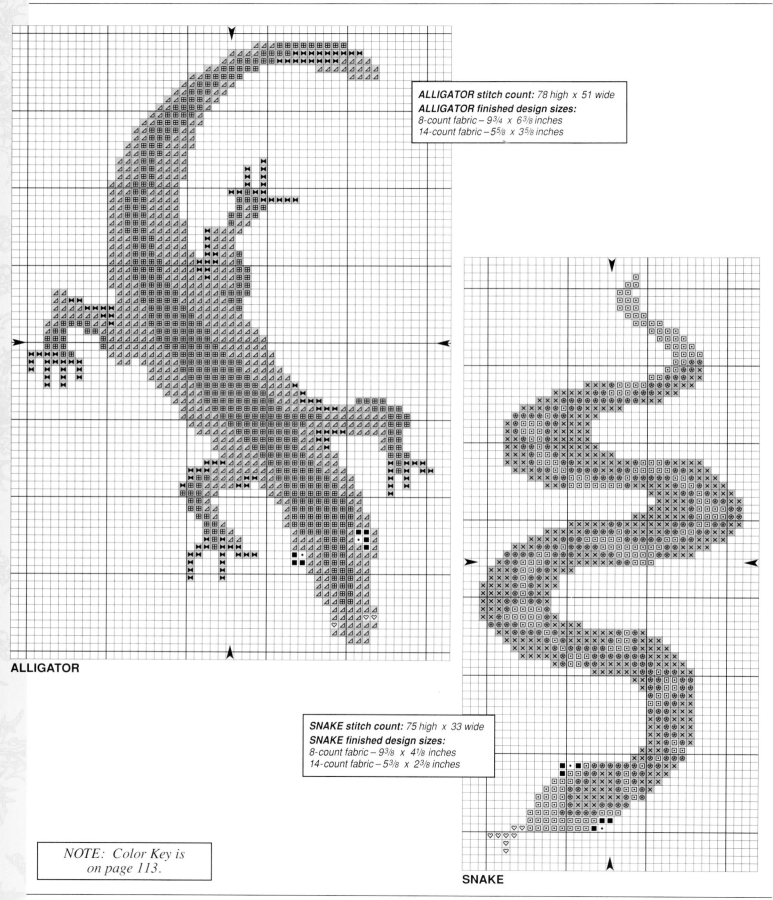

ALLIGATOR stitch count: 78 high x 51 wide
ALLIGATOR finished design sizes:
8-count fabric – 9 3/4 x 6 3/8 inches
14-count fabric – 5 5/8 x 3 5/8 inches

ALLIGATOR

SNAKE stitch count: 75 high x 33 wide
SNAKE finished design sizes:
8-count fabric – 9 3/8 x 4 1/8 inches
14-count fabric – 5 3/8 x 2 3/8 inches

*NOTE: Color Key is
on page 113.*

SNAKE

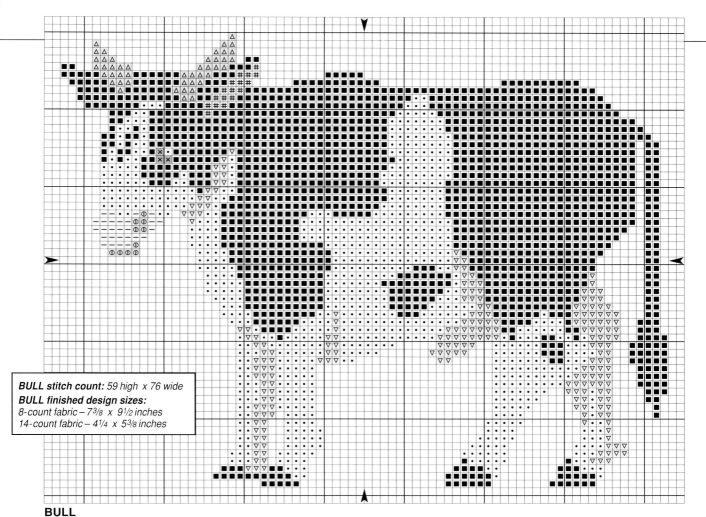

BULL stitch count: 59 high x 76 wide
BULL finished design sizes:
8-count fabric – 7³/₈ x 9¹/₂ inches
14-count fabric – 4¹/₄ x 5³/₈ inches

BULL

CAMEL stitch count: 49 high x 71 wide
CAMEL finished design sizes:
8-count fabric – 6¹/₈ x 8⁷/₈ inches
14-count fabric – 3¹/₂ x 5 inches

CAMEL

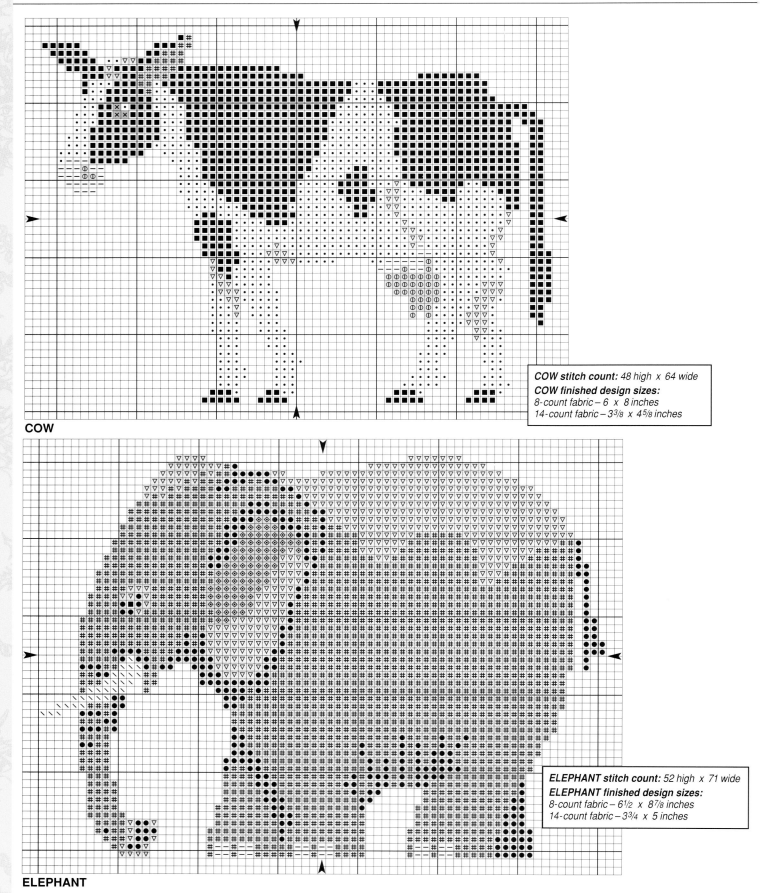

COW

COW stitch count: 48 high x 64 wide
COW finished design sizes:
8-count fabric – 6 x 8 inches
14-count fabric – 3³/₈ x 4⁵/₈ inches

ELEPHANT

ELEPHANT stitch count: 52 high x 71 wide
ELEPHANT finished design sizes:
8-count fabric – 6¹/₂ x 8⁷/₈ inches
14-count fabric – 3³/₄ x 5 inches

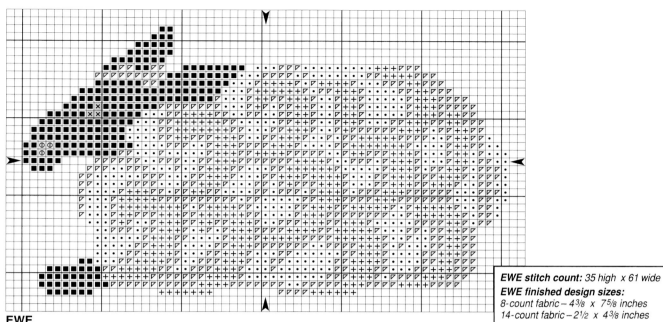

EWE

EWE stitch count: *35 high x 61 wide*
EWE finished design sizes:
8-count fabric – 4 3/8 x 7 5/8 inches
14-count fabric – 2 1/2 x 4 3/8 inches

STALLION

STALLION stitch count: *53 high x 55 wide*
STALLION finished design sizes:
8-count fabric – 6 5/8 x 6 7/8 inches
14-count fabric – 3 3/4 x 4 inches

NOTE: Color Key is
on page 113.

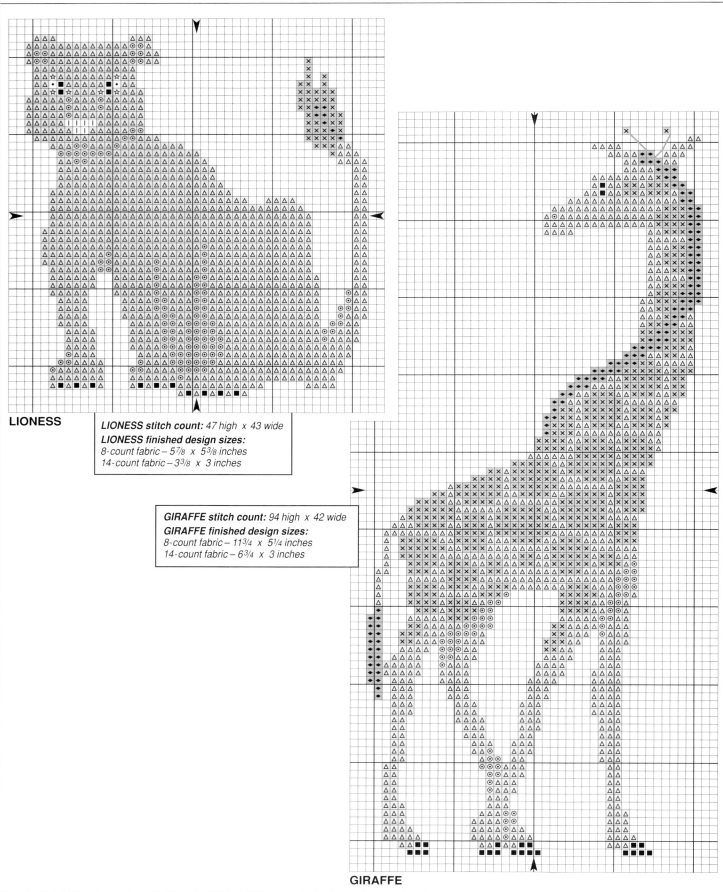

LIONESS

LIONESS stitch count: 47 high x 43 wide

LIONESS finished design sizes:
8-count fabric – 5⁷⁄₈ x 5³⁄₈ inches
14-count fabric – 3³⁄₈ x 3 inches

GIRAFFE stitch count: 94 high x 42 wide

GIRAFFE finished design sizes:
8-count fabric – 11³⁄₄ x 5¼ inches
14-count fabric – 6³⁄₄ x 3 inches

GIRAFFE

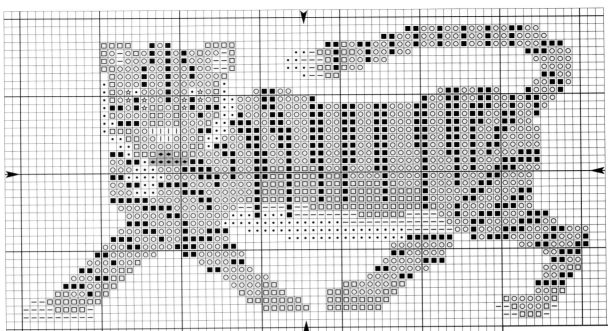

TIGER

TIGER stitch count: *38 high x 71 wide*
TIGER finished design sizes:
8-count fabric – 4¾ x 8⅞ inches
14-count fabric – 2¾ x 5 inches

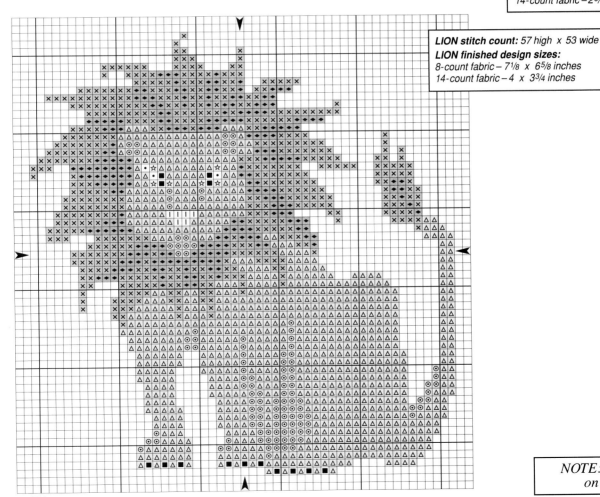

LION stitch count: *57 high x 53 wide*
LION finished design sizes:
8-count fabric – 7⅛ x 6⅝ inches
14-count fabric – 4 x 3¾ inches

LION

NOTE: Color Key is on page 113.

All Through the House

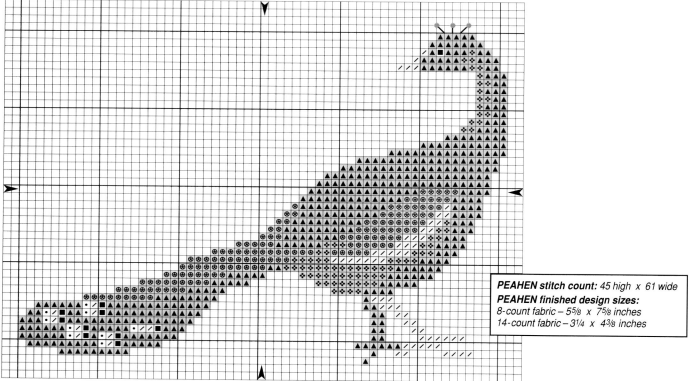

PEAHEN

PEAHEN stitch count: 45 high x 61 wide
PEAHEN finished design sizes:
8-count fabric – 5⅝ x 7⅝ inches
14-count fabric – 3¼ x 4⅜ inches

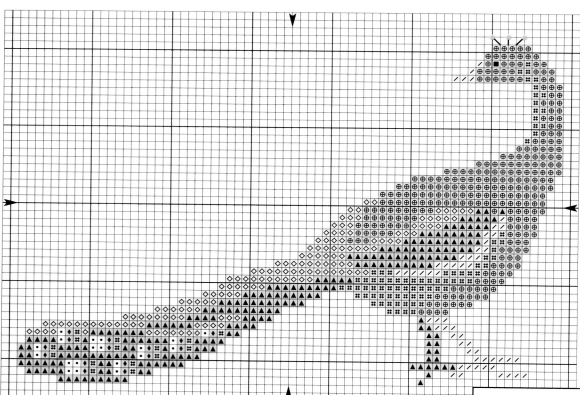

PEACOCK

PEACOCK stitch count: 46 high x 68 wide
PEACOCK finished design sizes:
8-count fabric – 5¾ x 8½ inches
14-count fabric – 3¼ x 4⅞ inches

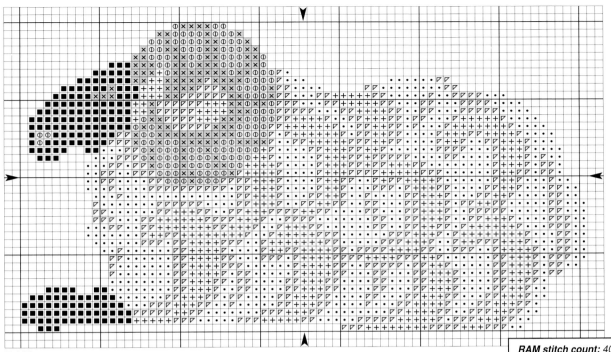

RAM

RAM stitch count: 40 high x 71 wide
RAM finished design sizes:
8-count fabric – 5 x 8⅞ inches
14-count fabric – 2⅞ x 5 inches

MARE stitch count: 53 high x 55 wide
MARE finished design sizes:
8-count fabric – 6⅝ x 6⅞ inches
14-count fabric – 3¾ x 4 inches

MARE

*NOTE: Color Key is
on page 113.*

CROSS-STITCH BASICS

Getting started

Cut the floss into 15- to 18-inch lengths and separate all six plies. Recombine the plies as indicated in the project instructions and thread into a blunt-tipped needle. Rely on the project instructions to find out where to begin stitching the piece.

Basic cross-stitch

Make one cross-stitch for each symbol on the chart. For horizontal rows, stitch the first diagonal of each stitch in the row. Then, work back across the row, completing each stitch. On most linen and evenweave fabrics, stitches are worked over two threads as shown in the diagram, *below*. For Aida cloth, each stitch fills one square.

Cross-stitches also can be worked in the reverse direction. Just remember to embroider the stitches uniformly; that is, always work the top half of the stitch in the same direction.

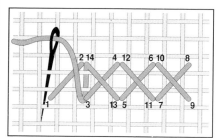

Basic Cross-Stitch in Rows

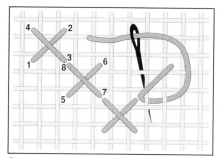

Basic Cross-Stitch Worked Individually

How to secure thread at beginning

The most common way to secure the beginning tail of thread is to hold it under the first four or five stitches.

Or, you can use a waste knot. Thread needle and knot end of thread. Insert needle from right side of fabric, about 4 inches away from placement of first stitch. Bring needle up through fabric and work first series of stitches. When stitching is finished, turn piece to right side and clip the knot. Rethread needle with excess floss and push needle through to the wrong side of stitchery.

When you work with two, four, or six plies of floss, use a loop knot. Cut half as many plies of thread, but make each one twice as long. Recombine plies, fold the strand in half, and thread all the ends into the needle. Work the first diagonal of the first stitch, then slip the needle through the loop formed by folding the thread.

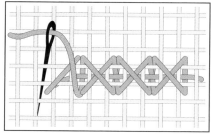

How to Secure Thread at Beginning

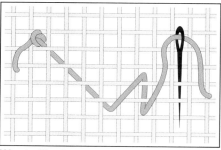

Waste Knot

How to secure thread at end

To finish, slip threaded needle under previously stitched threads on wrong side of fabric for four or five stitches, weaving thread back and forth a few times. Clip thread.

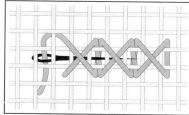

How to Secure Thread at End

Half stitches

A half cross-stitch is simply a single diagonal or half of a cross-stitch. Half cross-stitches are usually listed under a separate heading in the color key and are indicated on the chart by a diagonal colored line in the desired direction.

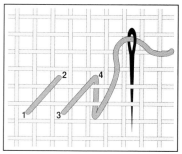

Half Cross-Stitch

Quarter and three-quarter stitches

Quarter and three-quarter stitches are used to obtain rounded shapes in a design. On linen and evenweave fabrics, a quarter stitch extends from the corner to the center intersection of threads. To make quarter stitches on Aida cloth, you'll have to estimate the center of the square. Three-quarter stitches combine a quarter stitch with a half cross-stitch. Both stitches may slant in any direction.

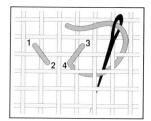

Quarter Cross-Stitch

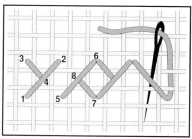

Three-Quarter Stitch

Cross-Stitches with beads

When beads are attached using a cross-stitch, work half cross-stitches and attach beads on the return stitch.

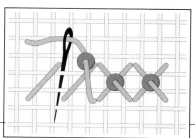

Cross-Stitch with Bead

Backstitches

Backstitches are added to define and outline the shapes in a design. For most projects, backstitches require only one ply of floss. On color key, (2X) indicates two plies of floss, (3X) indicates three plies, etc.

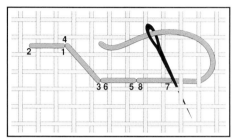

Backstitch

French knot

Bring threaded needle through fabric and wrap floss around the needle as illustrated. Tighten the twists and insert needle back through same place in the fabric. The floss will slide through the wrapped thread to make the knot.

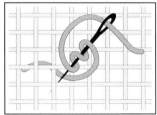

French Knot

Whipstitch

A whipstitch is an overcast stitch which is often used to finish the edges on projects that use perforated plastic. The stitches are pulled tightly for a neatly finished edge. Whipstitches can also be used to join two fabrics together.

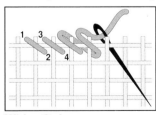

Whipstitch

CHART RATING

The rating system tells the degree of difficulty for each design. Find the star next to the project title.

Easy	★
Experienced	★★
Skilled	★★★
Expert	★★★★

MATERIALS FOR CROSS-STITCH

Counted cross-stitch has become a popular form of stitchery. Many stitchers like to work cross-stitch designs on different fabrics and use different threads than specified in the projects. Here is some information to help you understand the projects in this book and adapt them to your own special needs.

Cross-stitch fabrics

Counted cross-stitch can be worked on any fabric that will enable you to make consistently sized, even stitches.

Aida cloth is the most popular of all cross-stitch fabrics. The threads are woven in groups separated by tiny spaces. This creates a pattern of squares across the surface of the fabric and enables a beginning stitcher to easily identify exactly where the cross-stitches should be placed. Aida is measured by squares per inch; 14-count Aida has 14 squares per inch.

Aida cloth comes in many varieties. 100% cotton Aida cloth is available in thread counts 6, 8, 11, 14, 16, and 18. 14-count cotton Aida cloth is available in over 60 colors. For beginners, white Aida is available with a removable grid of pre-basted threads.

Linen is considered to be a standard of excellence fabric for experienced stitchers. The threads used to weave linen vary in thickness, giving linen fabrics a slightly irregular surface. When you purchase linen remember that the thread count is measured by threads per inch, but most designs are worked over two threads, so 28-count linen will yield 14 stitches per inch. Linens are made in counts from 14 (seven stitches per inch) to 40.

Evenweave fabric is also worked over two threads. The popularity of cross-stitch has created a market for numerous specialty fabrics for counted cross-stitch. They are referred to as evenweave fabrics because they are woven from threads with a consistent diameter, even though some of these fabrics are woven to create a homespun look. Most evenweave fabrics are counted like linen, by threads per inch, and generally worked over two threads.

Hardanger fabric can be used for very fine counted cross-stitch. The traditional fabric for the Norwegian embroidery of the same name has an over-two, under-two weave that produces 22 small squares per inch.

Needlepoint canvas is frequently used for cross-stitching, especially on clothing and other fabrics that are not suitable alone. Waste canvas is specially designed to unravel when dampened. It ranges in count from 6½ to 20 stitches per inch. Cross-stitches can also be worked directly on mono needlepoint canvas. It is available in colors, and when the background is left unstitched, it can create an interesting effect.

Sweaters and other knits are often worked in duplicate stitch from cross-stitch charts. Knit stitches are not square, they are wider than they are tall. A duplicate-stitched design will appear broader and shorter than the chart it was worked from.

Gingham or other simple plaid fabrics can be used, but gingham "squares" are not perfectly *square*, so a stitched design will seem slightly taller and narrower than the chart.

Burlap fabric can easily be counted and stitched over as you would on a traditional counted-thread fabric.

Threads for stitching

Most types of thread available for embroidery can be used for counted cross-stitch projects.

Six-ply cotton embroidery floss is available in the widest range of colors, including variegated colors. Six-ply embroidery floss is made to be separated easily into single or multiple plies for stitching. Instructions with each project in this book will tell you how many plies to use. If you change to a different fabric, use the chart, *page 126*, as a guide and experiment on a corner of the fabric until you achieve the effect you want. A greater number of plies will result in a rich or heavy embroidered piece, few plies create a lightweight or fragile texture.

Rayon and silk floss is very similar in weight to cotton floss, but stitches have greater sheen. Either thread can be interchanged with cotton floss, one ply for one ply, but because they have a "slicker" texture, they are slightly more difficult to use.

Pearl cotton is available in four sizes: #3, #5, #8, and #12. (#3 is thick; #12 is thin.) It has an obvious twist and a high sheen.

Flower thread is a 100% cotton, matte-finish thread. A single strand of flower thread can be substituted for two plies of cotton floss.

Overdyed threads are being introduced on the market every day. Most of them have an irregularly variegated "one-of-a kind" appearance. Cotton floss, silk floss, flower thread, and pearl cotton weight threads are available in this form. All of them produce a soft shaded appearance without changing thread colors.

Specialty threads can add a distinctive look to cross-stitch work. They range in weight from hair-fine blending filament, usually used with floss, to ⅛-inch-wide ribbon. Specialty threads include numerous metallic threads, richly colored and textured threads, and fun-to-stitch, glow-in-the-dark threads.

Wool yarn, usually used for needlepoint or crewel embroidery, can be used for cross-stitch. Use one or two plies of three-ply Persian yarn. It is best to select evenweave fabrics with fewer threads per inch when working cross-stitches in wool yarn.

Ribbon in silk, rayon, and polyester becomes an interesting texture for cross-stitching, especially in combination with flower-shaped embroidery stitches. Look for straight-grain and bias-cut ribbons in solid and variegated colors and in widths from ¼₆ to 1½ inches.

Types of needles
Blunt-pointed needles are best for working on most cross-stitch fabrics because they slide through holes and between threads without splitting or snagging the fibers. A large-eyed needle accommodates the bulk of embroidery threads. Many companies sell such needles labeled "cross-stitch," but they are identical to tapestry needles, blunt tipped and large eyed. The chart, *above,* will guide you to the right size needle for most common fabrics.

One exception to the blunt-tip needle rule is waste canvas; use sharp embroidery needles to poke through the fabric.

Working with seed beads requires a very fine needle to slide through the holes. Either a #8 quilting needle which is short with a tiny eye or a long beading needle with its longer eye are readily available. Some needlework shops carry short beading needles with a long eye.

FABRIC / NEEDLES / FLOSS

Fabric	Tapestry Needle size	Number of plies
11-count	24	Three
14-count	24-26	Two
18-count	26	Two
22-count	26	One

CROSS-STITCH TIPS

Preparing fabric
The edges of cross-stitch fabric take a lot of abrasion while a project is being stitched. There are many ways to keep fabric from fraying while you stitch.

The easiest and most widely available method is to bind the edges with masking tape. Because tape leaves a residue that's almost impossible to remove, it should be trimmed away after stitching is completed. All projects in this book that include tape in the instructions were planned with a large margin around the stitched fabric so tape can be trimmed away.

There are some projects where you should avoid tape. If a project does not have ample margins to trim away tape, use one of the techniques listed in the next paragraph.

If you have a sewing machine readily available, zigzag stitching, serging or narrow hemming are both neat and effective. Hand overcasting also works well, but is more time consuming.

Garments, table linens, towels, and other projects that will be washed on a regular basis when they are finished, should be washed before stitching to avoid shrinkage later. Wash the fabric in the same manner you will wash the finished project.

Preparing floss
Most cotton embroidery floss is color-fast and won't fade. A few bright colors, notably reds and greens, contain excess dye that could bleed onto fabrics if dampened. To remove the excess dye before stitching, gently slip off paper bands from floss and rinse each color in cool water until the water rinses clear. Then place the floss on white paper toweling to dry. If there is any color on the toweling when the floss is dried, repeat the process. When completely dry, slip the paper bands back on the floss.

Centering the design
Most projects in this book instruct you to begin stitching at the center of the chart and fabric. To find the center of the chart, follow the horizontal and vertical arrows on the chart to the point where they intersect.

To find the center of the fabric, fold fabric in half horizontally, and baste along the fold. Fold fabric in half vertically and baste along fold. The point where basting intersects is the center of the fabric. Some stitchers like to add some additional lines of basting every ten or twenty rows as a stitching guide.

Cleaning your work
You may want to wash your needlecraft pieces before framing. The natural oils from your hands eventually will discolor the stitchery so it's a good idea to remove those oils before mounting and framing. Wash your piece by hand in cool water using mild detergent. Rinse several times, until the water is clear.

Do not wring or squeeze to get the water out. Hold the piece over the sink until dripping slows, then place flat on a clean terrycloth towel and roll tightly. Unroll the stitchery and lay flat to dry.

Pressing finished work
Carefully press the fabric from the back before framing or finishing. If the piece has lots of surface texture stitches, place it on a terrycloth towel or other padded surface to press.

Framing your design
Use determines how cross-stitch pieces should be mounted and framed. Needlework shops, professional framers, and craft stores offer many options for both.

For most purposes, omit glass when framing cross-stitch. Moisture can build up between the glass and stitchery and sunlight is intensified by glass. Both can cause fabric damage. If you must use glass, be sure to mat the piece so the stitchery doesn't touch the glass.

INDEX

SOURCES / SUPPLIERS

Many of the materials and items used in this book are available at craft and needlework stores. For more information, write the manufacturers below.

Chapter 1

Guiding Star Tree Topper, pages 6–7: Perforated plastic—Darice, Inc., 2160 Drake Rd., Strongville, OH 44136; beads—Mill Hill Beads, 800/447-1332; metallic threads—Kreinik Manufacturing, 800/537-2166.
Frosted Snowflakes, page 8: Metallic threads—Kreinik Manufacturing.
Glorious Angel Tree Topper, page 9: Perforated plastic—Darice, Inc.; seed and bugle beads—Mill Hill Beads; metallic threads—Kreinik Manufacturing.
Festive Stocking Garland, pages 10–11: Perforated paper—Yarn Tree Designs, 117 Alexander St., P.O. Box 274, Ames, IA 50010, 515/232-3121.
Holly Jolly Tree Skirt, page 11: Tree skirt—Wichelt Imports, Inc., R.R. 1, Stoddard, WI 54658; ribbon—C.M. Offray & Sons, Inc., Route 24, Box 601, Chester, NJ 07930, 908/879-4700; Floralia wool yarn—DMC, Port Kearney Bldg. 10, South Kearney, NJ 07032-0650.
Lacy Hardanger Ornaments, page 12: Angel charm—Nordic Needle, Inc., 1314 Gateway Dr., Fargo, ND 58103, 800/433-4321, fax, 701/235-0952.
Scandinavian Mitten Ornaments, page 12: Beads—Mill Hill Beads.
Celestial Wonders, page 13: Perforated plastic—Darice, Inc.; metallic threads—Kreinik Manufacturing.

Chapter 2

Sweet Candy Train, page 28: Perforated plastic—Darice, Inc.; metallic threads—Kreinik Manufacturing.
Pretty Poinsettias and Brass Horn Tray and Coaster, pages 30–31: Wooden serving tray and coaster—Sudberry House, Box 895, Old Lyme, CT 06371.
Merry Bear Stacking Blocks, page 32: Perforated paper—The Yarn Tree.
Rat-a-tat Toy Soldier, page 33: Perforated plastic—Darice, Inc.; Marlitt rayon floss—Susan Bates, Div. of Coats and Clark; beads—Mill Hill Beads; metallic threads—Kreinik Manufacturing; ribbon—C.M. Offray & Sons, Inc.

Chapter 3

Cookie Jar Stocking, page 42: Navy Lugana fabric—Zweigart, 2 Riverview Dr., Somerset, NJ 08873-1139, 908/271-1949; cord—Heritage Trimming, Parade Hill Rd., Barnstead, NH 03218, 603/435-6795; piping—Hollywood Trims, 42005 Cook St., Suite 106, Palm Desert, CA 92260; beads—Mill Hill Beads.
Cookie Jar Ornaments, page 43: Perforated plastic—Darice, Inc.; ribbon—C.M. Offray & Sons, Inc.
Southwestern Stocking and Ornaments, page 44: Barrel beads and copper buttons—The Beadery, P.O. Box 178, Hope Valley, RI 02832; gold piping—Hollywood Trims.
Scandinavian Stocking, page 45: Jubilee fabric—Zweigart; piping—Hollywood Trims.
Jester Stocking, page 46: Cord—Heritage Trimming.

Chapter 4

Merry Yule Sampler and Kitchen Accessories, pages 58–59: Iron-on transfer pen—Sulky of America, 3113 Broadpoint Dr., Harbor Heights, FL 33983, 813/629-3199.
Fly-Fishing Case, pages 60-61: Perforated plastic—Darice, Inc.
Snow Family Finger Puppets, page 66: Perforated plastic—Darice, Inc.
Bluebird Bear, page 67: Metallic threads—Kreinik Manufacturing.

Chapter 5

Snowflake Vest, page 82: Vest—Hickory Hollow, P.O. Box 95, Versailles, KY 40383; RibbonFloss—Rhode Island Textile Co., Pawtucket, RI 02862.
Snowman, Santa, and Angel Pins, page 83: Perforated paper—The Yarn Tree; beads—Mill Hill Beads.
Tasseled Treasures Necklace and Earrings, page 84: Metallic threads—Kreinik Manufacturing; perforated paper—The Yarn Tree.
Christmas Party Cummerbund, Button Covers, and Earrings, pages 84–85: Metallic cord, #8 braid, gold torsade trim, and pailletes—Kreinik Manufacturing.
Reindeer Sweater, page 86: Sweater—Land's End, 800/356-4444.
Sweetheart Holiday Collar, page 87: Linen collar—Charles Craft, 800/277-0980.
Friendship Mittens, page 88: Mittens—Isotoner Gloves, 417 Fifth Ave., New York, NY 10016; RibbonFloss—Rhode Island Textile Co.

Chapter 6

Tidings of Joy Sampler and Tree Base, pages 98–99: Flower thread—DMC, Port Kearney Bldg. 10, South Kearney, NJ 07032-0650; metallic threads—Kreinik Manufacturing.
Tidings of Joy Place Mat, page 98: Silveretta place mat—Zweigart; metallic threads—Kreinik Manufacturing.
Tidings of Joy Ornaments, page 98: Perforated paper—The Yarn Tree; metallic threads—Kreinik Manufacturing.
Santa's Wish, page 100: Gold metallic thread—DMC.
Christmas Music Bellpull, page 101: Metallic threads—Kreinik Manufacturing; cord—Heritage Trimming.
Noah's Ark Quilt, page 102: Grosgrain ribbon—C.M. Offray & Sons, Inc.
Noah's Ark Tree Topper, page 103: Perforated plastic—Darice, Inc.

FABRICS

Charles Craft, P.O. Box 1049, Laurinberg, NC 28353, 800/277-0980; Wichelt Imports Inc., R.R.1, Stoddard, WI 54658; Zweigart, 2 Riverview Dr., Somerset, NJ 08873-1139, 908/271-1949.

THREADS

Anchor, Consumer Service Dept., P.O. Box 27067, Greenville, SC 29616; DMC, Port Kearney Bldg. 10, South Kearney, NJ 07032-0650; Kreinik Manufacturing, 800/537-2166.

Framing: Dot's Frame Shop, 4223 Fleur Dr., Des Moines, IA 50321.
Flowers: Boesen the Florist, 3801 Ingersoll, Des Moines, IA 50312.
Santa Claus: Harold Morine, 505 SE 8th St., Ankeny, IA 50021, 515/964-3785.